The 500
BEST-VALUE
WINES *in the* LCBO

∽ 2017 ∾

The 500

BEST-VALUE

WINES *in the* LCBO

━━━━━━━━━━━━━━

2017

{
THE DEFINITIVE GUIDE
TO THE BEST WINE DEALS
IN THE LIQUOR CONTROL
BOARD OF ONTARIO
}

Rod Phillips

UPDATED NINTH EDITION

whitecap

EDITED BY Patrick Geraghty
INTERIOR DESIGN BY Grace Partridge
COVER DESIGN BY Grace Partridge and Andrew Bagatella
TYPESET BY Andrew Bagatella

Printed in Canada

❦

Cataloguing data available from Library and Archives Canada.

ISBN: 978-1-77050-315-1

We acknowledge the financial support of the Government of Canada through the
Canada Book Fund (CBF) for our publishing activities and the Province of British
Columbia through the Book Publishing Tax Credit.

Nous reconnaissons l'appui financier du gouvernement du Canada et la province de
la Colombie-Britannique par le Book Publishing Tax Credit.

Canada

17 18 19 20 21   5 4 3 2 1

CONTENTS

The Reds

PREFACE TO THE 2017 EDITION

This is a guide to the best-value wines within the wide range available in LCBO (Liquor Control Board of Ontario) stores throughout Ontario (even if you're not in Ontario, chances are you'll find many of these wines available where you live.) There are so many good- to great-value wines available at reasonable prices in the LCBO, and it's a pity not to take advantage of them. If you tend to buy the same few wines time after time, this list will help you broaden your horizons and reduce the risk in being adventurous. If you're already adventurous, you're sure to find wines here that you haven't tried.

To compile this list of 500 wines, I tasted nearly all the wines available in the LCBO, and my ratings and reviews point you to wine styles you'll easily recognize. Each wine is ranked out of five stars (see How I Rate the Wines on page 5), but you should read the description of each wine. Stars tell you one critic's assessment of the quality of wine, but they don't tell you what any wine is like or if you'll like it. If you don't like sweet wines, you won't like an icewine that's rated 5 stars any more than one rated 4 stars.

I hope you find this book a useful guide to discovering wines you enjoy. If you come across a wine that's not listed here but that you think should be included in the next edition, please let me know. You can reach me at rodphillips@worldsofwine.com.

Cheers!

THANKS

Once again, I thank all the wine agencies and individual wineries, together with everyone in their sales, communications, and marketing teams, for providing the wines I tasted for this book. It's a lot of time, work, and expense to get the wines together, and then to ship or deliver them to me, and I really appreciate the cooperation I get every year.

I also wish to thank the Liquor Control Board of Ontario for inviting me to their regular tastings of Vintages, Vintages Essentials, and new LCBO wines.

Again, it was a pleasure to work with the people at Whitecap Books who make my job so easy, Patrick Geraghty, Nick Rundall, and Andrew Bagatella.

WHAT'S NEW IN THE 2017 EDITION

More than a hundred of the wines in this book are new entries. Some are wines the LCBO added to its portfolio since the last edition appeared. Others have been in the LCBO longer, but made the grade this year. That means, of course, that an equal number of the wines in last year's edition are not here. Some have been delisted by the LCBO, while I decided that others just didn't perform as well in my tasting for this edition. There are concentrations of new entries in Chilean and South African white wines, and Argentine, Australian, Californian, Chilean, French, and Ontario red wines, as well as in the sparkling wines and sherry sections.

But many of the wines here are veterans that have been in the LCBO for years. This is not a bad thing, as most of them stay on the shelves because they're good wines, reliable vintage after vintage, and consistently supported by consumers. After re-tasting almost the whole LCBO inventory, I've changed some ratings. Although most LCBO wines don't vary much from vintage to vintage, some do, and I've made some changes accordingly.

Overall, the quality of wines in the LCBO has been rising steadily. The 2008 edition of this book, the first year of publication, included wines rated from three to five stars. By the 2011 edition, there were very few three-star wines. In this edition, as in the previous one, there are none; all wines here are rated four, four-and-a-half, or five stars in value. That means the top third of wines in the LCBO and Vintages Essentials lists has steadily risen in quality and value. There's just no need to buy mediocre and poor-value wines.

SOME WINE TRENDS TO WATCH FOR

Rosé wines continue to increase in number and popularity, and they're drunk year-round, rather than only in the summer. France is leading the way with rosé: almost a third of all wine consumed there is rosé. No longer just pink and sweet, the new breed of varietally labelled rosés tend to be dry and well made, although there are also good off-dry rosés too. Starting in spring, the LCBO brings in "seasonal volumes" (often quite limited volumes) of rosés that aren't available year round, but I think there's enough interest to justify a much better year-round selection.

The LCBO is providing a better selection of sparkling wines year after year. Sparkling wine has escaped from the celebration ghetto as people realize that sparkling wine (including champagne) is not only for anniversaries, weddings, birthdays, and the like, but for everyday drinking. The range of sparkling wine in this book grows each year.

New World wine-producing countries increasingly want us to think in regional, not simply national, terms. They want us to go looking for a wine from South Australia, Barossa Valley, or Margaret River, not just for "an Australian wine." In this year's list, for example, you'll see fewer Australian wines from South Eastern Australia, the huge zone that accounts for the bulk of Australia's wine production. Many wines that used to be designated as coming from there are now shown as coming from either individual states (like South Australia or New South Wales) or smaller regions, like Mudgee or Langhorne Creek. The same tendency of identifying wines by smaller regions can be seen in California, Chile, and Argentina.

Finally, we await the arrival of the new big wine—the wine that will sweep the wine world as New Zealand sauvignon blanc, Australian shiraz, and Argentine malbec did. There's more and more Spanish garnacha (grenache) available. Could that be the next big red? Or might it be cabernet franc, a variety that's widely planted and increasingly appreciated?

HOW I DESCRIBE THE WINES

The most common way of describing wines, especially in North America, is to use fruit, spices, and other produce (and things) as references. We've all seen wines described as having aromas and flavours like "red cherry, plum, and black pepper, with notes of leather" or "tropical fruit, peach, and citrus." I call these "Carmen Miranda" reviews. (Carmen Miranda was the Brazilian singer famous for her hats covered with exotic fruit.) Sometimes reviewers get even more specific and find flavours such as "Damson plums, ripe Red Delicious apples, and Bing cherries, with nuances of finely ground green peppercorns."

Very few people can distinguish these flavours in wine, although it's a skill that many can learn. But even though it's possible to discern these aromas and flavours, no wine ever really tastes primarily like a combination of cherry, plum, and black pepper (just imagine it), or of tropical fruit, peach, and citrus (you're better off drinking fruit juice, if that's what you're looking for). There might be hints or reminders of these flavours in the wine, but they're details. Just watch professionals swirling and sniffing (sometimes favouring one nostril over the other) as they strain to pick up and identify the most subtle and fleeting aromas.

Focusing on these nuances misses the big picture. In this book I focus on the main characteristics of each wine and on its style: Is it light, medium, or full bodied? Are the flavours intense, concentrated, or understated? Is it simple and fruity or well structured? Is it dry, off-dry, sweet, or very sweet? Is it tannic or not? Does it have a smooth, tangy, juicy, or crisp texture? These are the most important qualities of any wine, whether you're looking for a wine to sip on its own or one to go with a specific food.

Most of us describe wine in these terms. We say we like red wine that's dry, full bodied, and rich, white wine that's off-dry, light, and refreshing, or rosé that's slightly sweet. And when we're looking for wine to go with dinner, we might think of an intensely flavoured, full-bodied red for steak, or a lighter white or crisp rosé for a summer salad.

What we *don't* look for is a wine with flavours of black plums or raspberries, or notes of red grapefruit, black pepper, or honey. And we certainly don't say we love wines with flavours of wet stones, forest floors, smoky tar, or hard-ridden horses—the sort of descriptions loved by some wine reviewers.

In short, you'll find that the reviews in this book describe wines in the common-sense way in which most people think of them.

3

THE LCBO'S SWEETNESS SCALE

The LCBO provides a convenient sweetness indicator for each wine, telling you where the wine sits on a spectrum from extra dry to sweet. The LCBO used to indicate the actual residual sugar levels in wine. (Residual sugar is the amount of sugar, usually expressed in grams per litre, after fermentation is finished. Dry wines may have no residual sugar or only one or two grams per litre, while very sweet wines, such as icewine, have hundreds.)

The current system is much more useful because it indicates how sweet the wine *seems,* regardless of the amount of residual sugar in it. That's really important, because sugar can be counteracted by acidity; if you taste two wines with the same level of residual sugar, the one with more acidity will taste less sweet than the one with less acidity.

The LCBO's "perceived sweetness" system is coded like this, and these are the letters you'll see for each wine in this book:

XD = Extra Dry: No perceived sweetness; clean, crisp acidic finish

D   = Dry: No distinct sweetness; well-rounded, balanced acidity

M   = Medium: Slight sweetness perceived

MS = Medium Sweet: Noticeably sweet

S   = Sweet: Distinctly sweet

As examples, most cabernet sauvignons and pinot noirs are XD and most chardonnays and pinot grigios are D, but icewines, of course, are S. Nearly all the wines in this book are XD or D. When the LCBO web site doesn't show the perceived sweetness of a wine, I've given my own rating, and I've also noted cases where I disagree with the LCBO's rating.

If you still want to know the actual sugar level—as some people do for health reasons—it's shown for each wine on the LCBO's website.

HOW I RATE THE WINES

I tasted not only all the wines listed in this book, but about another thousand available in the LCBO and Vintages Essentials lists. As far as I know, I'm the only person who tastes almost all these wines in a short period (I do it in four weeks), and this gives me a unique perspective on them.

I taste the reds at a cool temperature—the way they should be served—and the whites, rosés, and sparkling wines chilled, but not cold.

The 500 wines in this book are the ones I consider the best in terms of their intrinsic quality and value. The quality of a wine depends on the balance among its various components (flavour profile, residual sugar, acidity, alcohol, and tannins) and the complexity of its flavour, structure, and texture. (Like most reviewers, I don't pay much attention to colour and length of finish—the time the flavours and texture remain in your mouth after you've swallowed the wine.) A wine that's well balanced and very complex scores higher than one with little complexity or poor balance.

All the wines in this book are good, very good, or excellent in quality, and the five-star rating reflects their value to the consumer. A $10 wine rated four-and-a-half stars is better value than a $10 wine rated four stars. But value can be found at all price levels. A $30 wine rated four stars has a quality level that is very good value for its price.

Here's what my star system means:

★ ★ ★ ★ ★   It's hard to imagine better value at this price. This wine is very well balanced and very complex.

★ ★ ★ ★ ½   Excellent value at this price. The wine is well balanced with a good level of complexity.

★ ★ ★ ★   Very good value at this price. The wine is well balanced and complex.

★ ★ ★ ½   Above-average value at this price. The wine has fair levels of balance and complexity.

★ ★ ★   Good value at this price. The wine is well made but might lack much complexity.

Indicates that the wine is new to this edition.

BRAND OR WINERY

RATING (*out of five*)

GRAPE VARIETY

VINTAGE YEAR

NEW!
★ ★ ★ ★

La Mascota Cabernet Sauvignon 2011

MENDOZA $14.40 (292110) 12.5% ALC. **D**

Argentina produces many fine cabernet sauvignons, which go as well with the country's beef-heavy diet as the better-known malbecs. This full-bodied cabernet is quite rich, with plush and concentrated flavours and a generous and smooth texture. It has enough acidity to suit it to food, though, and it's a natural for well-seasoned red meats.

NOTES

....

....

....

....

[Vintages Essential] *indicates the wine is found in the Vintages section, or at a Vintages store.* [Non-vintage] *indicates that the wine doesn't show a year on its label.*

LCBO PRODUCT CODE

ALCOHOL CONTENT

REGION

LCBO SWEETNESS INDICATOR

PRICE
(*per 750 mL bottle, unless otherwise indicated*)

ABOUT THE LCBO

The LCBO (including Vintages, its fine-wine arm) sells more than 80 percent of the wine purchased in Ontario, and its wine sales total more than $1.6 billion a year. The remaining wine sales are made by winery-owned retail stores, online merchants, and agents and wineries who sell directly to restaurants, bars, and individual clients. The LCBO is where most Ontarians shop for wine because it has so many locations and offers the biggest range of imported and Canadian wine in the province.

Critics of the LCBO often complain that its wine selection is too limited, but most consumers find it bewilderingly large. That's the reason for this book. It guides you to the best-value wines in the LCBO. The others are in Vintages stores or Vintages sections of the LCBO. This book also includes many of the wines continuously available in the Vintages Essentials collection, which numbers about 100.

It can sometimes be a challenge to locate a particular wine in the LCBO. There are more than 600 LCBO stores throughout the province, plus more than 200 small agencies in isolated localities, and the range of wine varies widely from outlet to outlet. The main LCBO stores in major cities carry nearly all the LCBO's wines, while others have a more limited selection on hand.

In the unlikely event that you forget to bring this book along when you go wine shopping, you can ask an LCBO Product Consultant for help. They have passed LCBO wine-knowledge exams and know the LCBO's and Vintages' inventories well.

If you see a wine in this book that you'd like to try but that isn't available at your local LCBO, call the liquor board's helpline at 1-800-ONT-LCBO (1-800-668-5226). An agent will tell you the nearest store that has the wine you're looking for. Alternatively, use the search engine at www.lcbo.com to find a wine and identify the LCBO stores close to you that have it.

Bear in mind that the LCBO's inventory is constantly changing. New wines are added and others are dropped. Prices change, too, according to currency exchange fluctuations and other factors. The prices in this book were correct when it went to press.

The vintages of wines in the LCBO also change as one vintage sells out and is replaced by the next. You might see a 2013 wine listed here and find that the 2014 vintage is on the LCBO shelf. For the most part, there's little variation from vintage to vintage in LCBO wines, and it's generally safe to go with my reviews and ratings even when the vintage is different.

BUYING, SERVING, AND DRINKING WINE:
SOME COMMON QUESTIONS

Are wines sealed with a screw cap poorer quality than wines sealed with a cork?
Not at all. In fact, some of the best-known and most reliable producers
seal all their still wines, including their top brands, with screw caps.
There's some debate about the use of screw caps on wines intended for
long-term aging, but there's no doubt at all that they are excellent for
wines meant to be drunk within five or six years of being made—like
all the wines in this book. On the other hand, natural corks can contain
bacteria capable of mildly or seriously tainting wine, although the
incidence of "corked" wines is far lower than it was ten years ago. Corks
can also produce variability from bottle to bottle, whereas wines sealed
with screw caps are almost always more consistent. Are screw caps the last
word in wine-bottle closures? Probably not, as experiments are ongoing
with other types of seals.

Are wines in boxes and plastic bottles poorer quality than wines in glass bottles?
There's a common misconception that only inferior wine is sold in boxes
(like TetraPak cartons) or bottles made of plastic (such as PET, a food-
grade plastic that does not taint the contents). You can't generalize about
the quality of wine based on its packaging—after all, there are plenty of
poor wines in glass bottles. In practice, though, many producers put their
lower-quality wines in boxes and plastic. The only reason excellent wine
might not be sold in such packaging is that there's some question about
how long it preserves wine in good condition. The LCBO experimented
with wines in TetraPak and PET some years ago, but almost all LCBO
wines are now in glass bottles.

Are more-expensive wines better than cheaper ones?
In very broad terms, there is often a relationship between quality and
price. High-quality wine demands high-quality grapes (which are often
more expensive to grow or buy) and may involve more expenses in
production, such as the use of oak barrels. But although it's not as easy
to find a great wine under $10 or $15 as it is to find one over $20 or $30,
this book shows that there are plenty of high-quality and very good-value
wines at reasonable prices.

Are wine labels a good guide to what's inside the bottle?

Labels are an important part of marketing wine. Wine is no different from other products, and producers expect that consumers will often be drawn to a particular wine by its packaging—and that usually means the label. Labels can be sophisticated (like those on many expensive and ultra-premium wines), fun (like most of the labels featuring animals), and even provocative (like the Fat Bastard brand). The fact that all are represented in this book shows that there's no necessary link between the label and quality or value. But beyond projecting an image, labels provide consumers with important information. Depending on where the wine is from, the label tells the grape variety (or varieties) used to make the wine and/or where the grapes were grown. The label also tells you the vintage and the alcohol level, and it might give information such as whether the wine is organic, kosher, or fair trade. Some of this information might be on a back label along with a description of the wine, the production process or the producer. But bear in mind that any description of the wine on the back label is written by the producer to promote sales.

Does the serving temperature of wine make any difference?

The serving temperature of wine matters a lot because it affects qualities in the wine such as flavour and texture (the way the wine feels in your mouth). Too many people (and restaurants) serve white wine too cold and red wine too warm. White wines are refreshing when they're chilled, but most should not be served straight from the fridge. Wine that's too cold has little flavour, so take white wine out of the fridge 15 or 20 minutes before you serve it. Red wine, on the other hand, should be served cooler than it usually is—especially in restaurants where the wine is stored on shelves in the dining room. Red wine should feel cool in your mouth, and that means cooler than the 20°C or higher of most homes and restaurants. (The guideline of serving red wine "at room temperature" is not very useful if you like to live in sauna-like temperatures.) If your red wine is too warm, it will feel coarse and flabby and won't have the refreshing quality that makes wine such an ideal partner for food. To cool red wine that's too warm, put it in the fridge for 15 to 20 minutes before serving. Remember, it's better to serve any wine too cool than too warm; it will warm up quite quickly in your glass.

How many different kinds of wine glasses do I need?

If you look in wine accessory, kitchen, and even many department stores, you'll see a wide selection of wine glasses in many different shapes and sizes, often classified by grape variety. Do you really need one glass for chardonnay, another for merlot, and yet another for shiraz? No, you don't. Although the shape and size of the glass can sometimes highlight the qualities in different wines, you can enjoy nearly all from one or two different glasses. In general, most people prefer to drink wine from finer glasses than from thicker-sided tumblers or glasses. Look for glasses that are wider toward the bottom of the bowl, and fill the glass only to the widest point. That gives room for the aromas to collect. And if you're interested in tasting wine as judges and professionals do, buy some tasting glasses at a wine accessories store. They're smaller than most wine glasses, wide at the bottom and tapered toward the mouth (like the stylized glasses on the cover of this book), and they bring out the aromas and flavours of wines very well. One style of wine often drunk from a specific glass is sparkling wine. It's frequently served in a tall, slender glass (called a flute) that shows off the bubbles to the best effect, but many professionals prefer to drink sparkling wine from a bigger, wider glass.

Should I let wine "breathe" before I serve it?

There's a common belief that wine should be opened and left standing to "breathe" for an hour or two before being served. It's based on the theory, which is true, that most wine improves after being exposed to air for a short time. But simply opening a bottle of wine exposes a very small amount of wine (the dime-size surface in the neck of the bottle) to air, and it makes no perceptible difference to the wine. Pouring the wine into glasses as soon as you open the bottle exposes the wine to air far more effectively than letting it stand in the open bottle for hours. You can also decant wine to expose it to air, and that raises the question . . .

Do I need to decant wine?

There are two reasons to decant wine. The first is to pour the wine without disturbing the sediment that has collected in the bottom of the bottle so that you can make sure it doesn't get into your glass. Of course, this is necessary only when there's sediment present, and that's rarely the case with wines made for early drinking (like virtually all the wines in this book). The second reason to decant does apply to the wines here—in fact, it applies to any wine, whether red, white or rosé—and that's to expose the wine to some air before you drink it. This is more accurately called "aerating" than "decanting," and it generally improves the aromas, flavours, and texture of wine, and therefore its overall quality. You needn't buy an expensive decanter (there are many on the market for less than $15), but look for one with a broad mouth and a wide bottom. If you don't have a decanter at hand but want to aerate a bottle of wine, pour it into a clean bottle (or a pitcher) and then back into the original bottle.

What do I do with leftover wine?

Opened wine lasts longer if you keep it in the refrigerator and longer still if you minimize exposure to air. Just re-corking or screwing the cap back on a half-finished bottle leaves the wine exposed to a lot of air, so it's better to pour leftover wine into a smaller container, like a clean half-bottle, where there's little or no air between the surface of the wine and the top of the bottle. If you're keeping a half-full bottle, store it standing up, rather than on its side, so that the surface exposed to air is minimal. Kept in the fridge like this, leftover wine should be good for at least two or three days. If you have leftover sparkling wine, use a dedicated stopper; they're available for a few dollars at wine accessory stores.

Does wine improve with age? Should I have a wine cellar?

While some wines (called "vins de garde") are made for aging, almost all the world's wine is made for drinking as soon as it's released for sale. It will not improve with age in the bottle; instead, it will eventually deteriorate and become undrinkable. Most consumers buy wine as they need it, but there's no reason why you shouldn't keep a number of bottles of wine on hand. For that purpose, you don't need a proper cellar with controlled temperature and humidity, but your wine will keep best if it's in a dark, cool place (ideally between 10°C and 15°C). The corner of a basement, a closet, or the space under a staircase might be suitable, but a kitchen counter, where the wine will be exposed to light and heat, is not. Wine kept in too-warm conditions eventually develops a "stewed" character. If you want to store a few dozen or more bottles of vins de garde so that they improve over a longer term, check the internet or a wine accessory store for information on wine cabinets or how to build a wine cellar.

MATCHING WINE AND FOOD

Matching food with wine is not nearly as difficult as many people think—or are led to think by too many wine professionals who make it sound like rocket science. Ignore the complicated treatises that tell you that a smoky note in this wine echoes a hint of smoke in that dish. Similarly, ignore the food and wine matching guides and apps that tell you to pair this food with that wine. Both food and wine vary widely—there's no *one* chicken curry and no *one* pinot gris—so you're better off following your own common sense.

That said, a few basic guidelines can help you choose a pairing that does what it should: enhance your enjoyment of both the food and the wine. What you most want to avoid is a pairing where one overwhelms or interferes with your enjoyment of the other. For example, a full-flavoured wine will smother food that has delicate flavours, and sweet food can make dry wines taste sour. The best pairing leaves the food tasting the way the cook intended and the wine the way the winemaker planned.

Matching wine and food should be fun. Each review in this book includes a food match that works well, but don't take them too literally. Each suggestion represents a style. A wine that goes with beef will almost always team equally well with lamb and other red meats, and one that pairs successfully with chicken will also marry happily with turkey.

Some basic guidelines:
- Match heavier dishes (like red or hearty meat, or vegetable stews) with medium- to full-bodied wines and lighter dishes (like salads and white fish) with light- to medium-bodied wines. The weight of food often comes from sauces. White fish alone is light, but a cream sauce makes it heavier.

- Focus on the style of the entire dish, not just the main item. The overall flavour of unseasoned roast chicken is mild. But chicken in a spicy, rich tomato sauce has more complexity.

- Herbs and spices give richer and more complex texture to food. Barbecued pork has more complexity than unseasoned pork, for example, and a wine that pairs well with richly flavoured food will match it better.

- Focus on the style of the wine, not only its colour. For the purpose of matching food, a full-bodied, rich, oaked chardonnay might have more in common with a red wine than with a light-bodied, delicate white.

ARGENTINA

ARGENTINA IS THE FIFTH-LARGEST wine producer in the world. It became a major wine exporter only in the 2000s, but quickly earned a reputation for producing quality wines at prices that offer very good value. Although better known for its red wines (especially malbec), Argentina produces many excellent whites. One of the most interesting white grapes is torrontés, which has become Argentina's signature white variety. It generally shows pungent aromas and a crisp, refreshing texture. Other whites are made from popular varieties like chardonnay and pinot grigio.

Most Argentine wine is labelled by the sprawling Mendoza region, although some is starting to be labelled by Mendoza's smaller sub-regions, such as the Uco Valley. Other important wine regions are San Juan, Salta/Cafayate in the far north, and Patagonia in the south.

Crios Torrontés 2015

★ ★ ★ ★ ★

MENDOZA $13.95 (1834) 13.5% ALC. D

[Vintages Essential] Made by Susana Balbo, one of Argentina's foremost winemakers, this delicious, well-made torrontés is easy-drinking on its own and pairs well with white fish and poultry dishes. Look for very attractive flavours from start to finish, underpinned by bright and refreshing acidity. It's an excellent example of a popular style of this too-little known grape variety.

NOTES

....
....
....
....

FuZion 'Alta' Torrontés/Pinot Grigio 2015

★ ★ ★ ★

MENDOZA $9.95 (168419) 13% ALC. D

The torrontés variety deserves to be much better known and appreciated, and maybe harnessing it to pinot grigio will help. The result here is a richly aromatic wine that shows lovely concentrated flavours that are defined and quite complex. It's zesty and fresh, and an excellent choice for spicy Asian-influenced dishes that feature pork, poultry, or tofu.

NOTES

....
....
....
....

FuZion Chenin/Chardonnay 2015

★ ★ ★ ★

MENDOZA $8.05 (119800) 12.5% ALC. D

When FuZion frenzy first hit Ontario, the object of mass adoration was the shiraz/malbec. Since then, the Zuccardi family, which owns the winery, has added more varieties, including this attractive white. It delivers very pleasant flavours that are full and fruity, and they come with a fresh, crisp texture that makes for easy drinking. Enjoy it on its own or with spicy chicken or seafood. It's a natural for Asian dishes.

NOTES

....
....
....
....

Lurton 'Piedra Negra' Pinot Grigio 2014

★ ★ ★ ★

VALLE DE UCO, MENDOZA $12.95 (556746) 12.5% ALC.   **XD**

Lurton is an unusual company in that it makes wine under the same name in many countries. This pinot grigio from its Argentine winery in Mendoza delivers quite delicious and intense aromas and flavours. It's plush, mouth-filling, and quite stylish, and has food-friendly edginess. It's a terrific choice for sipping alone or drinking with spicy seafood, chicken, or much Asian cuisine.

NOTES

....

....

....

....

NEW!
★ ★ ★ ★ ½

Norton 'Barrel Select' Sauvignon Blanc 2015

MENDOZA $13.10 (400564) 12.5% ALC.   **D**

A small percentage of this sauvignon was aged in oak barrels, and it's just enough to add some complexity to the texture and flavours, bringing the wine toward a style known as "fumé blanc." You find a bit more weight than many sauvignons and plenty of layered nuances in the fruit. The typical sauvignon acidity is there, making this a great partner for smoked or grilled fish, seafood, and poultry dishes.

NOTES

....

....

....

....

WHITE WINES

AUSTRALIA

AUSTRALIA GRABBED THE ATTENTION of international wine drinkers in the 1990s and, despite some ups and downs, it still has a good grip. Although better known for red wine, especially shiraz, it produces a wide range of whites, too. The most common white variety in Australia is chardonnay, but others, such as the popular semillon/sauvignon blanc blend, also cross the Pacific Ocean to Ontario stores.

The regional designation found on many Australian wine labels is South Eastern Australia, a huge zone that includes more than 90 percent of Australia's wine production and most of its designated wine regions. But Australian wineries are now stressing the importance of specific regions, rather than just grape variety, in understanding their wines. In this list of Australian whites you'll find wines from state-designated regions such as Victoria and New South Wales, but also from less-known appellations like Adelaide Hills, Mudgee, and Central Ranges.

Deakin Estate Viognier 2014

★★★★ ½

AUSTRALIA $10.00 (399253) 13.5% ALC. **D**

This is a really lovely, easy-drinking viognier that shows plenty of ripe fruit and excellent fruit-acid balance. The flavours are rich and generous, with plenty of discernible complexity and they're supported by crisp, clean acidity. It's essentially dry, and goes with poultry, pork, and seafood, but the fruitiness suits it to spicier dishes, too.

NOTES

....
....
....
....
....

George Wyndham 'Bin 222' Chardonnay 2014

★★★★

SOUTH EASTERN AUSTRALIA $12.95 (93401) 13% ALC. **XD**

So many chardonnays . . . and yet some stand out from the crowd. This is one. Your first impression will be the smoothness of the texture. It seems to glide effortlessly across your palate, filling your mouth with concentrated and nuanced flavours as it does so. For all that, it's more than just fruity, and it has all the refreshing acidity needed for chicken, salmon, turkey and pork.

NOTES

....
....
....
....

Jacob's Creek Reserve Chardonnay 2014

★★★★ ½

ADELAIDE HILLS $14.95 (270017) 12.1% ALC. **XD**

Jacob's Creek is a small tributary that flows into the Chardonnay River—in a vinous sense, not geographically. Here you find an attractive chardonnay with layered, ripe flavours that hold solid right through the palate. The texture is round and smooth, with tanginess to keep your palate awake. Sip it on its own or drink it with roast or grilled chicken, turkey or pork, or with medium-strength cheeses.

NOTES

....
....
....
....

Lindemans 'Bin 65' Chardonnay 2015

★ ★ ★ ★

SOUTH EASTERN AUSTRALIA $11.10 (142117) 13.5%   D

Bin 65 was designed specifically for the Canadian market because of the
popularity of this style of wine there. Launched in 1985, it quickly became
an icon throughout the world. Year after year, it delivers solid, ripe fruit
flavours, a clean, smooth, and slightly edgy texture, and good balance.
It isn't too much of anything but has enough of everything to make it a
versatile food wine. Drink it with roast pork or chicken.

NOTES

....

....

....

....

McWilliam's 'Hanwood Estate' Chardonnay 2013

★ ★ ★ ★ ½

NEW SOUTH WALES $14.10 (557934) 13.5% ALC.   XD

This medium-bodied chardonnay gets marks for elegance in addition to
its other positive qualities. It delivers rich and complex flavours with a
subtle hint of oak, and everything is lifted by the remarkably refreshing
and clean texture. It's fruity but dry, and it's an excellent choice when
you're serving chicken, fish, pork, or perhaps seafood in a cream sauce.

NOTES

....

....

....

....

....

Penfolds 'Koonunga Hill' Chardonnay 2013

★ ★ ★ ★ ½

SOUTH AUSTRALIA $16.15 (321943) 13.5% ALC.   XD

Dr. Christopher Penfold started making wine in Australia in the 1840s
and prescribed it to his settler patients for the anemia many suffered after
their long voyages from Britain. Now we drink it for pleasure, and you
can certainly enjoy the intense, ripe fruit flavours in this chardonnay. It's
medium bodied and very well balanced, and has a rich, attractive texture.
Drink it with roast pork or turkey.

NOTES

....

....

....

....

tic tok pocketwatch Chardonnay 2014

★ ★ ★ ★ ½

CENTRAL RANGES $15.20 (187104) 12.5% ALC.   D

From the Central Ranges wine region of New South Wales, this is a well-made chardonnay that combines weight and elegance. The fruit is concentrated and plush, but it shows good structure and complexity, and the well-calibrated acidity shines through fresh and clean. This is several cuts above most chardonnays, and it's very versatile. Drink it with white fish and seafood, or with poultry and pork.

NOTES

....

....

....

....

NEW!
★ ★ ★ ★ ½
Wolf Blass 'Gold Label' Chardonnay 2013

ADELAIDE HILLS $25.15 (399543) 12.5% ALC.   XD

This is a stylish chardonnay that's interesting to drink with its "Yellow Label" sibling (below). Both are well made and worthy, but you can see the shift in the quality of the components and their interactions. (I guess gold has that relationship to yellow.) The fruit is deliciously focused and layered, and the acidity is finely calibrated. The balance is spot-on. You can also drink this with fish, chicken, or pork, to help you drink both together.

NOTES

....

....

....

....

★ ★ ★ ★
Wolf Blass 'Yellow Label' Chardonnay 2015

PADTHAWAY/ADELAIDE HILLS $15.10 (226860) 13% ALC.   XD

Wolf Blass "Yellow Label" cabernet sauvignon was Wolfie's first big hit in Ontario, and now LCBO shelves have more of his mellow-yellow labels. The fruit is forward and this style of chardonnay has wide appeal. What gives it quality and value are the complexity of the flavours and the refreshing acidity, which make this a great choice for fish, chicken, or pork dishes.

NOTES

....

....

....

WHITE WINES

AUSTRIA

AUSTRIA HAS A well-established wine industry and its wines are widely appreciated, but we seldom see them in Ontario. White wines are Austria's forte, and its signature variety is grüner veltliner.

Winzer Krems 'Sandgrube 13' Grüner Veltliner 2014

NIEDERÖSTERREICH $13.10 (375022) 12% ALC.   D

This grüner veltliner is made in a popular, easy-drinking style. It shows quite delicate fruit flavours that are backed by crisp and clean acidity. It's on the lighter side of the spectrum and its fresh character makes it an excellent candidate if you're looking for a wine to sip without food. But it also goes well with white fish, seafood, chicken, and mild cheeses.

NOTES

....

....

....

....

BRITISH COLUMBIA

BRITISH COLUMBIA'S WINERIES produce many quality and value-priced white wines, but you won't find very many on LCBO shelves. Don't blame the LCBO. The reason is that British Columbians love their wine and drink most of what's made in their province. Much of the rest is sold in western Canada and the US states to the south of British Columbia, rather than being shipped to Ontario.

The Vintners Quality Alliance (VQA) classification on British Columbia wine labels means that the grapes were grown in the region specified and that the wine has been tested and tasted by a panel.

Mission Hill Reserve Chardonnay 2014

★ ★ ★ ★ ½

VQA OKANAGAN VALLEY $21.95 (545004) 13.5% ALC.   XD

[Vintages Essential] Mission Hill is the Okanagan Valley's iconic winery, a tourist destination that attracts crowds to see its architecture and its site, and to taste its well-made wines. This chardonnay is rich and elegant with intense, upfront fruit flavours and a smooth, mouth-filling texture. It's nicely balanced with the crispness needed to make it work well with food. Try it with grilled salmon or roast pork.

NOTES

....

....

....

....

CALIFORNIA

A WIDE RANGE OF WHITE GRAPES grows in California's vineyards, but the state is best known for chardonnay, its most popular and widely planted variety. Still, don't overlook other quality whites, especially pinot grigio and sauvignon blanc. Napa Valley is California's most famous region, but others like Sonoma County, North Coast, and Central Coast, as well as smaller appellations like Paso Robles, Alexander Valley, and Lodi, are becoming better known to consumers. Some California white wines are designated simply "California," which means that producers can source grapes from any region throughout the state, without having to change the appellation every time they draw grapes from a different region.

Beringer 'Founders' Estate' Chardonnay 2014

★ ★ ★ ★ ½

CALIFORNIA $17.95 (534230) 13.9% ALC.   D

The "founders" here are the Beringer brothers, Jacob and Frederick, who founded the winery in the 1870s. They'd be proud of this chardonnay, which delivers so well in every respect. The flavours are rich, well defined, and complex, while the texture is plush, smooth, and round. Clean acid adds juicy freshness, and the result is a wine you can enjoy with well-seasoned chicken, pork, and white fish dishes.

NOTES

....

....

....

....

Beringer 'Founders' Estate' Pinot Grigio 2014

★ ★ ★ ★ ½

CALIFORNIA $17.15 (45641) 13% ALC.   D

This very attractive pinot grigio delivers real stylishness and elegance, vintage after vintage. The flavours are well defined with both concentration and delicacy, and the texture shows a beautiful balance of acidity and fruit. It's silky smooth and has a refreshing quality that suits food, although you could savour it on its own, too. If you're thinking of pairing this with a meal, try a delicately spiced Thai dish.

NOTES

....

....

....

....

Big House 'The Birdman' Pinot Grigio 2014

NEW!
★ ★ ★ ★

CALIFORNIA $13.10 (237271) 12.5% ALC.   D

In the tradition of Big House wines, puns abound on the labels of this wine. "Pretensions fly away when paired with grilled seafood or Asian cuisine," it reads. Good pairings, I agree, although the grammar could use work. This is a lovely, fruity, fresh-textured pinot grigio that makes for easy drinking. There's nothing too serious about it; it's all about enjoyment, with or without food.

NOTES

....

....

....

....

Chateau St. Jean Chardonnay 2014

★ ★ ★ ★ ★

SONOMA COUNTY $18.95 (269738) 13.6% ALC. XD

This is an elegant chardonnay that shows ripe, vibrant fruit right through the palate and through a long finish. The flavours are generous, complex, and verging on plush, with the oak enhancing the texture without interfering with the fruit purity. The acidity is clean, fresh, and juicy. With terrific balance, this goes beautifully with richer chicken, pork, fish, and seafood dishes.

NOTES

....

....

....

....

NEW! Clos du Bois Chardonnay 2013

★ ★ ★ ★

NORTH COAST $15.95 (400549) 13.5% ALC. D

This is a big, generous, and mouth-filling chardonnay that goes very well with poultry, pork, and many seafood dishes, as well as with mild or lightly smoked cheeses. The flavours are positive and nicely layered, and the acid-fruit balance is very good. The oak is well managed: it's perceptible but not obtrusive and certainly doesn't interfere with the purity of the fruit.

NOTES

....

....

....

....

Conundrum White 2014

★ ★ ★ ★ ★

CALIFORNIA $24.95 (694653) 13.5% ALC. M

[Vintages Essential] This delicious off-dry blend of white grapes includes chardonnay, sauvignon blanc, viognier, and muscat. Muscat makes its presence felt on the nose and palate, and semillon contributes some richness to the texture. Overall, it's aromatic and full flavoured, with excellent balance. It has the fruitiness to handle many spicy dishes, but don't rule out roast chicken and pork.

NOTES

....

....

....

....

Enigma Chardonnay 2014

NEW!
★ ★ ★ ★

CALIFORNIA $13.95 (428854) 13.5% ALC. **D**

If you like a chardonnay with ripe-sweet fruit (there's also little residual sugar) and a little toastiness from the oak treatment, test drive this one. It delivers a texture that's smooth and inviting, along with decent complexity and a good acid-fruit balance. You can sip this on its own or pair it easily with chicken, pork, and white fish, not to mention summer salads and mild cheeses.

NOTES

....
....
....
....

Ghost Pines 'Winemaker's Blend' Chardonnay 2013

NEW!
★ ★ ★ ★ ½

SONOMA, MONTEREY, AND NAPA COUNTIES

$19.95 (308122) 14% ALC. **D**

This is a blend of wines from three different regions, each of which adds its character to the final wine. The winemaker is responsible for the final selection and percentages (hence the name) and the result here has impressive complexity and balance. This chardonnay stands above almost all others at its price point (and some that are more expensive). It's a terrific choice for many dishes featuring poultry, pork, white fish, and seafood.

NOTES

....
....
....

J. Lohr 'Riverstone' Chardonnay 2014

★ ★ ★ ★ ★

ARROYO SECO, MONTEREY $19.95 (258699) 13.5% ALC. **D**

[Vintages Essential] This is a stylish and opulent chardonnay from the little-known Arroyo Seco wine region in central California. Here you get plush, ripe, and multi-faceted fruit flavours that sit harmoniously with a texture that's full, round, and refreshing. It's dry and medium bodied and very well balanced. Enjoy this with herbed roast chicken, grilled salmon, pork tenderloin, or seared scallops or lobster.

NOTES

....
....
....

★ ★ ★ ★ ½

Kendall-Jackson 'Vintner's Reserve' Chardonnay 2014

CALIFORNIA $19.95 (369686) 13.5% ALC. D

[Vintages Essential] The oak treatment is evident on the nose and palate, but it's deftly executed so that the toastiness is integrated into the fresh fruit flavours. The flavours themselves are generous, forward without being assertive, and nicely layered, and they're complemented by clean, refreshing acidity. What's not to like? Pair this with roast or grilled pork or chicken.

NOTES

....

....

....

....

....

★ ★ ★ ★

Ménage à Trois White 2014

CALIFORNIA $16.95 (308015) 13.5% ALC. D

Made (of course) from three grape varieties—chardonnay, moscato, and chenin blanc—this is a wine you can enjoy on its own or with food. For the latter, good pairings would be chicken, turkey, or pork, or slightly spicy Asian dishes that feature these ingredients. Look for aromatic flavours that are consistent right through, as well as the good acid-fruit balance that gives this wine a refreshing character.

NOTES

....

....

....

....

NEW!
★ ★ ★ ★

Mirassou Pinot Grigio 2014

CALIFORNIA $14.45 (274480) 12.5% ALC. D

This is an attractive pinot grigio that goes well with a range of food, including poultry, mild cheeses, white pizza, and mild curries. The flavours are concentrated yet have some delicate qualities, and the acid-fruit balance is very good; this is a refreshing white that you can pair with food or drink on its own.

NOTES

....

....

....

....

Robert Mondavi Chardonnay 2013

★ ★ ★ ★ ★

NAPA VALLEY $26.25 (310409) 13.5% ALC.   **XD**

This is an elegant chardonnay with a winning combination of plush and quite intensely flavoured fruit and clean, fresh acidity. The fruit-acid balance is right on, and while the brightness of the acidity makes for a juicy texture that makes you think of food, the weightiness of the whole effort suits it for richer varieties of seafood (such as lobster, scallops) or cream-based seafood, fish, or white meat dishes.

NOTES

....

....

....

....

Robert Mondavi 'Private Selection' Chardonnay 2014

★ ★ ★ ★ ½

CENTRAL COAST $16.95 (379180) 13.5% ALC.   **XD**

Try this on any chardonnay-skeptic—that is, anyone who loudly declares that he or she doesn't like chardonnay, as if that's something to be proud of. Chardonnay comes in so many styles, and this is a particularly attractive one. It's almost full bodied and has a smooth texture and lovely concentrated flavours. It's a versatile, fruit-forward chardonnay that goes as well with roast chicken as it does with grilled salmon.

NOTES

....

....

....

....

Robert Mondavi 'Private Selection' Sauvignon Blanc 2014

★ ★ ★ ★

CENTRAL COAST $17.15 (405753) 13.5% ALC.   **XD**

This is a very good sauvignon blanc for food, and I'd be happy to drink it with white fish, seafood with a spritz of lemon, or lemon chicken, as well as with many poultry dishes and not-too-hot curries. Talk about versatile! It doesn't have the flavour power of most sauvignon blancs from New Zealand, but it's very consistent, attractive, and well balanced, and it has the refreshing and clean texture you look for in this variety.

NOTES

....

....

....

....

Sebastiani Chardonnay 2012

★ ★ ★ ★ ½

SONOMA COUNTY $19.95 (364497) 13.5% ALC.   **D**

Almost completely chardonnay (1.2 percent is made up of viognier, roussanne, and other white varieties to add some complexity), this is a delicious white that goes well with many poultry, pork, and richer seafoods (such as lobster and scallops). There's a veneer of toasty oak on the well-measured fruit, which is complex and well structured. Look for some juiciness from the acidity. In all, it's a well-integrated chardonnay and well suited for dining.

NOTES

....

....

....

....

Sterling 'Vintner's Collection' Chardonnay 2014

★ ★ ★ ★

CENTRAL COAST $16.00 (669242) 13.5% ALC.   **D**

This is a fairly classic West Coast style of chardonnay, with hints of oak in the aromas and the flavours. But, far from being overbearing, the oak is well managed and lets the rich fruit of the flavours shine through. The acidity is well balanced and all the components are well integrated. This is a very good choice for many richer poultry and pork dishes, as well as for smoked fish.

NOTES

....

....

....

....

Toasted Head Chardonnay 2014

★ ★ ★ ★ ½

CALIFORNIA $18.95 (594341) 13.5% ALC.   **D**

[Vintages Essential] "Toasted Head" refers to the practice of charring the insides of barrels. Often the ends (heads) are not toasted, but in the barrels used to age this chardonnay they were. This is a bold and assertive chardonnay with intense flavours and a round texture, but it carries the liveliness needed to pair well with food. Drink it with grilled salmon, pork tenderloin, or herbed roast chicken.

NOTES

....

....

....

Wente 'Morning Fog' Chardonnay 2014

★ ★ ★ ★ ½

LIVERMORE VALLEY/ $18.15 (175430) 13.5% ALC.   D
SAN FRANCISCO BAY

The morning fog is important to many California wine regions. It swirls up the river valleys at dawn and keeps the vines cool until it eventually dissipates in the late morning or early afternoon. The results are chardonnays like this that retain wonderful freshness of flavour and texture while having concentrated fruit and a round, silky mouth feel. It's a delicious wine with chicken, turkey, or pork.

NOTES

....

....

....

....

Woodbridge Sauvignon Blanc 2015

★ ★ ★ ★

CALIFORNIA $12.95 (40501) 13% ALC.   XD

There's a world of sauvignon blanc out there, from the big and pungent style popularized by New Zealand to the understated style more common in northern France. This inexpensive California example is vibrant and zesty, with nicely defined flavours that are bright and fresh. No question that this is destined for shellfish, seafood, or fish that's been subjected to a squeeze of fresh lemon.

NOTES

....

....

....

....

....

CHILE

ALTHOUGH CHILE IS BETTER KNOWN for its red wines, many of its whites deliver great quality and value. The warm growing conditions in most of Chile's wine regions have led many producers to seek out cooler areas (such as the Casablanca Valley) that are exposed to cold winds off the Pacific, and to plant grape vines at higher (and cooler) altitudes. The main white varieties planted are chardonnay and sauvignon blanc, but there are many others.

Designated Chilean wine regions are indicated by the letters DO *(Denominación de Origen)*. The grapes for wines that are simply designated "Chile" can be sourced from any region in the country.

Adobe Sauvignon Reserva Blanc 2015

★ ★ ★ ★ ½

DO CASABLANCA VALLEY $13.10 (266049) 12.5% ALC. **XD**

The cool, sunny growing conditions of the Casablanca Valley promote fruit ripeness and acidity in grapes, and that's exactly what you get in this very attractive sauvignon blanc. The flavours are ripe and bright, and the acidity is fresh, crisp, and clean. It's in a light-medium style, and perfect for summer salads, grilled white fish, seafood, and lightly seasoned poultry.

NOTES

Caliterra Reserva Sauvignon Blanc 2015

★ ★ ★ ★ ½

DO CASABLANCA VALLEY $10.05 (275909) 13.5% ALC. **XD**

The regions generally considered best for sauvignon blanc are the Loire Valley in France and Marlborough in New Zealand, but Chile produces well-priced competition. This one has a crisp, refreshing texture and vibrant, fresh fruit flavours. It's medium bodied and goes well with a goat cheese salad or with fish or seafood (or fish and chips) juiced with fresh lemon.

NOTES

Casas del Bosque Reserva Sauvignon Blanc 2014

NEW!
★ ★ ★ ★ ½

DO CASABLANCA VALLEY $14.95 (974717) 12.5% ALC. **D**

[Vintages Essential] This is a delicious and quite elegant sauvignon blanc that goes well with oysters and seafood in general, as well as with simple dishes such as fish and chips. The flavours are bright and breezy, like the Casablanca Valley itself, and the acidity is clean and crisp. These components are very well integrated to make a wine that's flavourful and refreshing.

NOTES

NEW!
★ ★ ★ ★

Concha y Toro 'Casillero del Diablo' Reserva Sauvignon Blanc 2015

CHILE $11.95 (578641) 13% ALC. **D**

Look for well-defined and quite concentrated flavours in this attractive sauvignon, along with decent complexity and layering. They're supported by a good seam of zesty acidity that gives the wine some food-friendly juiciness. As for the food, the usual sauvignon suspects are in play: white fish, seafood, goat cheese, and lighter curries.

NOTES
....
....
....
....

★ ★ ★ ★ ★

Cono Sur 'Bicicleta' Viognier 2015

DO COLCHAGUA VALLEY $9.95 (64287) 13.5% ALC. **XD**

You can make this your go-to white when you're eating spicy Thai or Indian dishes. It has rich, delicious, sweet fruit flavours and a refreshing texture, all of which tend to tame the spiciness a little without interfering with the flavours. Or drink it on its own. Viognier is an underappreciated variety, and this one comes from a winery that not only produces very good wine across the board, but has also pioneered many sustainable practices in its vineyards.

NOTES
....
....
....
....

★ ★ ★ ★

Cono Sur 'Bicicleta' Chardonnay 2015

CHILE $10.45 (321448) 13.5% ALC. **XD**

The vineyards that produced this wine are mostly in the cool Casablanca Valley, where the sun ripens the grapes and the cool breeze from the Pacific Ocean allows acidity to develop. The result is a lovely, refreshing, well-balanced wine with sweet fruit flavours and very good complexity. Enjoy this with poultry, white fish, seafood, and pork.

NOTES
....
....
....

Errazuriz 'Estate Series' Sauvignon Blanc 2015

★ ★ ★ ★

DO ACONCAGUA VALLEY $13.95 (263574) 13.5% ALC.   XD

This is a lively and refreshing sauvignon from the cooler, coastal end of the Aconcagua Valley, where the grapes develop bright acidity. Their flavours are fresh and vibrant and the balanced acidity makes for a juicy texture that goes brilliantly with freshly shucked oysters, white fish drizzled with lemon, and many seafood and poultry dishes. Think of it, too, for Greek chicken with lemon and garlic.

NOTES

....

....

....

....

Errazuriz 'Max Reserva' Sauvignon Blanc 2014

★ ★ ★ ★ ½

DO ACONCAGUA COSTA $16.15 (273342) 13% ALC.   XD

This sauvignon shows very good weight and a fairly dense texture. The fruit is solid, layered, and consistent from start to finish, and the acidity that develops at the cool, coastal end of the valley shows through well, making this a refreshing, if substantial, white. Drink it with the usual sauvignon suspects like white fish and seafood, but also try it with medium-heat curries.

NOTES

....

....

....

....

Las Mulas Reserva Organic Sauvignon Blanc 2015

★ ★ ★ ★

DO CENTRAL VALLEY $12.95 (272609) 13% ALC.   D

This is made from organically farmed grapes. It's a very easy-drinking, medium-bodied sauvignon that you can enjoy on its own or pair with dishes as varied as summer salads, grilled chicken, white fish (and fish and chips), and seafood. It shows lovely bright and reasonably complex flavours that are underpinned by a broad seam of lively acidity.

NOTES

....

....

....

....

NEW!
★ ★ ★ ★

Montes 'Twins' White 2015

DO ACONCAGUA COAST $11.95 (440156) 13% ALC.   **D**

A blend of sauvignon blanc, chardonnay, and viognier, it could have been called "Triplets." It's a fresh, fruity, and easy-drinking white that is also very well balanced and structured. The complex fruit pairs brilliantly with the clean, crisp acidity, and this is a very good choice for white fish and seafood, chicken, and pork, including recipes that deliver some spiciness.

NOTES

....

....

....

....

....

NEW!
★ ★ ★ ★

Santa Rita Reserva Sauvignon Blanc 2015

DO CASABLANCA VALLEY $14.05 (275677) 13.5% ALC.   **XD**

Here's another quality sauvignon blanc from Casablanca Valley that shows the excellent growing conditions there. The flavours are quite concentrated and complex, consistent right through the palate, and supported by crisp, almost zesty acidity. It goes very well with oysters and seafood generally, and is very pleasant to sip on its own.

NOTES

....

....

....

....

FRANCE

HUNDREDS OF FRENCH WINE REGIONS produce whites from many different varieties of grapes. Some regions are closely associated with specific grape varieties, like Burgundy to chardonnay and Sancerre to sauvignon blanc, but others are not. You'll find a wide range of varieties and styles in this list.

French wine labels display a few terms worth knowing. Wines labelled *Appellation d'Origine Contrôlée* (abbreviated AOC in this book) or *Appellation d'Origine Protégée* (AOP) have the highest-quality classification in France. They're made under tight rules that regulate the grape varieties that can be used in each region, blending percentages, maximum crop yield, minimum alcohol levels, and so on.

Wines labelled *Vin de Pays* or IGP *(Indication Géographique Protégée)* are regional wines made with fewer restrictions. They must be good quality, but producers have much more flexibility in the grapes they can use and how much wine they can make per hectare of vineyards. *Vins de Pays d'Oc* (Oc is the ancient region of Occitanie) are by far the most common of the *Vins de Pays* wines.

Bouchard Père & Fils Mâcon-Lugny Saint-Pierre 2014

★ ★ ★ ★ ½

AOC MÂCON-LUGNY $17.95 (51573) 12.5% ALC.   XD

This is from a designated area in the Mâcon region in southern Burgundy. Made from 100 percent chardonnay, it's an elegant wine that delivers nicely concentrated flavours that are soft and stylish. The texture is quite rich and creamy, with a seam of acidity that makes it very refreshing. This is an excellent wine for grilled salmon and for meats like chicken, turkey, and pork.

NOTES
....
....
....
....

Bouchard Père & Fils Petit Chablis 2014

★ ★ ★ ★ ½

AOC PETIT CHABLIS $20.95 (51466) 12% ALC.   XD

Petit Chablis is one of the appellations (designated regions) of Burgundy's broader Chablis region and it's often overlooked, partly because of the low minimum alcohol. But this is ideal if you want a lower-alcohol wine, especially during summer's heat. The flavours are restrained but positive, focused, and well defined. It's very refreshing and makes a very good match for chicken, white fish, and seafood.

NOTES
....
....
....
....

Bouchard Père & Fils Pouilly-Fuissé 2013

★ ★ ★ ★ ★

AOC POUILLY-FUISSÉ $28.85 (56580) 13% ALC.   XD

Pouilly-Fuissé is a prestigious region in southern Burgundy that produces only white wine and grows only chardonnay. Don't expect to see this labelled as a chardonnay, though, as the regional name has all the cachet. This one is gorgeous and stylish, with pure, nuanced flavours and a beautifully smooth and clean texture. Medium weight and dry, it's a great choice for poultry, pork, fish, or seafood.

NOTES
....
....
....
....

François Lurton Sauvignon Blanc 2014

NEW!
★ ★ ★ ★ ½

AOC BORDEAUX $11.95 (250381) 12% ALC. XD

Sauvignon blanc is one of the approved white grapes of Bordeaux and here it's made in a popular, easy-drinking style. The fruit is bright and pure and it's backed by clean, vibrant, and well-balanced acidity. You can drink this on its own, but it goes really well with white fish (and fish and chips), oysters and other seafood, and light curries.

NOTES
....
....
....
....

Guy Saget Sancerre 2014

★ ★ ★ ★ ★

AOC SANCERRE $25.25 (319657) 12.5% ALC. XD

Sancerre, at the eastern end of the long Loire Valley wine region, is noted for its sauvignon blanc wines that are generally known by the name of the region, not the variety. This fine example offers the classic Sancerre qualities of restrained but concentrated flavours, good complexity, and a vibrant platform of fresh acidity. It's dry and harmonious, and is a great partner for many poultry and white fish dishes.

NOTES
....
....
....
....
....

Henri Bourgeois 'Les Baronnes' Sancerre 2013

★ ★ ★ ★ ★

AOC SANCERRE $25.95 (542548) 12.5% ALC. XD

[Vintages Essential] Sancerre is a notable appellation for sauvignon blanc, and Henri Bourgeois is one of the main producers. (He also established a winery in New Zealand's Marlborough, another region known for sauvignon blanc.) This wine delivers concentrated but restrained flavours, with impressive structure and complexity. The acidity shines through, and it's a great choice for many white fish and seafood dishes, as well as for chicken.

NOTES
....
....
....

Jaffelin Bourgogne Aligoté 2014

★ ★ ★ ★

AOC BOURGOGNE ALIGOTÉ $16.95 (53868) 12% ALC.   **XD**

Aligoté is a Burgundian grape variety that's perhaps best-known for the wine used with cassis in making the aperitif kir. But it also makes worthy wine in its own right, as this example shows. It delivers attractive, fairly understated flavours, with a quite taut but balanced texture from the acidity. It makes a very good accompaniment to grilled white fish, trout, and roast chicken.

NOTES
....
....
....
....

Joseph Drouhin 'Vaudon' Chablis 2014

★ ★ ★ ★ ½

AOC CHABLIS $24.25 (284026) 12.5% ALC.   **XD**

There are lovely ripe aromas on the nose here. When you get the wine into your mouth they are more understated, but they're positive, solid, and persistent right through to the finish, and they show plenty of complexity. The acidity is bright and fresh, lifting the fruit and setting you up for food. This is an excellent choice for grilled white fish, herbed roast chicken, and mild cheeses.

NOTES
....
....
....
....

La Chablisienne 'Les Vénérables' Vieilles Vignes Chablis 2012

★ ★ ★ ★ ★

AOC CHABLIS $24.95 (215525) 12.6% ALC.   **XD**

[Vintages Essential] There's no standard definition of "old vines" *(vieilles vignes),* but producers often use the term because older vines produce small quantities of higher-quality grapes. This is certainly a delicious and elegant chablis (made from chardonnay in the northern part of Burgundy), with stylish and nuanced flavours and a smooth, refreshing texture. Everything is in fine harmony and balance. Serve this with simply prepared fish, chicken, or pork dishes.

NOTES
....
....
....

Laroche 'Saint Martin' Chablis 2014

★ ★ ★ ★ ½

AOC CHABLIS $23.20 (289124) 12% ALC.   D

Domaine Laroche is one of the most prestigious producers of chablis. Made from chardonnay, this wine delivers quality from start to finish. Look for very attractive, elegant flavours that are focused and subtly layered, and a texture that's rich, refined, and fresh. This is an excellent choice for shellfish, seafood, white fish, and poultry.

NOTES
....
....
....
....

Louis Bernard Côtes du Rhône 2014

★ ★ ★ ★

AOC CÔTES DU RHÔNE $13.95 (589432) 12.5% ALC.   XD

Made from grenache blanc, bourboulenc and clairette, this dry, medium-bodied white blend delivers good quality across the board. The ripe flavours are consistent from start to finish, and they're very ably supported by a seam of acidity that makes the wine a palate-refreshing partner for food. Drink it with roast poultry or pork or with grilled white fish or seafood.

NOTES
....
....
....
....

Louis Latour Chardonnay 2013

★ ★ ★ ★

AOC BOURGOGNE $20.70 (55533) 13% ALC.   XD

Nearly all white wines from Burgundy are made from chardonnay (as the reds are made from pinot noir). They vary in style from lean and acidic to plump and fruity. This is a mid-range style, with concentrated and nuanced flavours, a round and smooth (but refreshing) texture, and very good balance. Drink it with chicken, turkey, and soft mild cheeses like brie and camembert.

NOTES
....
....
....
....

M. Chapoutier 'Belleruche' Côtes du Rhône 2014

★ ★ ★ ★ ½

AOC CÔTES DU RHÔNE $16.95 (245340) 13.5% ALC.   XD

White côtes du Rhônes are not as common as their red siblings, but they are generally well worth looking for. This one (a blend of the grenache blanc, clairette, and bourboulenc varieties) shows very concentrated flavours, with good complexity and structure balanced very well with crisp, clean acidity. It's a great choice for meals of chicken, turkey, pork, or white fish.

NOTES
....
....
....
....

Pierre Sparr Gewürztraminer 2014

★ ★ ★ ★

AOC ALSACE $16.95 (373373) 13% ALC.   D

Pierre Sparr is an Alsatian producer who does very well across his portfolio. This is a lovely, medium-bodied gewürztraminer with an opulent and plump texture that fills your mouth with flavour. As for those flavours, they're spicy, pungent, and rich, with complexity to spare. If you're looking for a sparring partner for this wine, try a spicy Asian (especially Thai) dish.

NOTES
....
....
....
....

Remy Pannier Muscadet Sèvre et Maine 2014

NEW!
★ ★ ★ ★

AOC MUSCADET SÈVRE $15.20 (13821) 12% ALC.   XD
ET MAINE

Muscadet, a region on the Loire River close to the Atlantic, produces France's go-to wine for seafood. Drink this one with oysters, mussels, or white fish and you'll see why. The flavours are delicate but properly concentrated so that they complement the food rather than dominate it. And the bright acidity makes for a texture that's lively and fresh.

NOTES
....
....
....
....

William Fèvre 'Champs Royaux' Chablis 2014

★★★★½

AOC CHABLIS $19.70 (276436) 12.5% ALC. XD

The classic wines from Chablis are chardonnays made and aged in stainless steel tanks rather than in oak barrels. They offer pure, well-defined, and complex fruit flavours, as this one does. It has a refreshing texture—not plush and mouth-filling, but very crisp and clean. It's medium bodied and an excellent match for seafood and shellfish. Try it with mussels steamed in white wine and herbs.

NOTES
....
....
....
....

Willm Réserve Gewürztraminer 2014

★★★★½

AOC ALSACE $17.05 (269852) 12.5% ALC. M

This is a rich, more-than-off-dry style of gewürztraminer that's so commonly produced in Alsace it's referred to as the "Alsatian style." Look for plush, luscious fruit flavours that are quite intense and lingering, along with a good burst of acidity that makes another glass more than likely. This is an excellent choice for spicy dishes, and this style of gewürztraminer is almost a classic pairing with Asian cuisine.

NOTES
....
....
....
....

Willm Réserve Riesling 2014

★★★★½

AOC ALSACE $14.95 (11452) 12% ALC. XD

[Vintages Essential] This is a lovely dry riesling with long, focused flavours that stay true right through the palate. They're supported by brisk, clean acidity that's refreshing and perfect for food. It's a very good choice for pork and chicken, but it also goes well with white fish and seafood and it has the acidity to handle oilier foods like smoked salmon.

NOTES
....
....
....
....
....

WHITE WINES

GERMANY

WONDERFUL, GOOD-VALUE GERMAN WHITE WINES appear
often in the LCBO's Vintages section, but although the selection
in the LCBO has improved a lot, it still doesn't deliver the best
Germany can deliver in value. Unfortunately, many people are
still reluctant to buy German wines because they believe they're
all sickly sweet. But most German wines are dry. While it's true
that many quality German wines do have some sweetness, it's not
fake and cloying. It comes from the richness of natural sugars in
the grapes, and these wines should have a regular place on your
table.

Important terms on German wine labels are *Prädikatswein* (the
highest-quality classification of wine) and *Qualitätswein* (wine of
high quality but not of the highest level). Each of these terms is
followed by the name of the wine region where the grapes were
grown.

NEW!
★★★★
Baden Gewürztraminer 2014

QUALITÄTSWEIN BADEN $11.90 (336735) 11% ALC.   **D**

This is a fairly dry gewürztraminer that shows the character associated with the variety. It's aromatic on the nose, with sweet and pungent aromas, and they flow through to the flavours, which are focused and consistent. The acidity keeps it bright and refreshing. This is a versatile gewürztraminer than goes well with many spicy Asian dishes, but pairs equally well with many Western poultry and vegetarian dishes, too.

NOTES

....
....
....
....

NEW!
★★★★ ½
Joseph Drathen Kabinett Gewürztraminer 2013

PRÄDIKATSWEIN $10.50 (394601) 10.5% ALC.   **M**
RHEINHESSEN

This is a very attractive gewürztraminer that strikes the right balance of sweetness, fruitiness, and acidity. The flavours are the classic pungent ones common to the variety, and although there's residual sugar here, it's reined in effectively by the bright, fresh acidity. Chill it down and drink it as an aperitif, or take it to the table and pair it with spicy dishes featuring pork, chicken, seafood, or vegetables.

NOTES

....
....
....
....

NEW!
★★★★★
Villa Wolf Riesling 2014

QUALITÄTSWEIN PFALZ $12.95 (394023) 11% ALC.   **M**

This wine is made by well-known producer Dr. Loosen. It's an off-dry riesling that delivers luscious, pungent flavours with depth and breadth. The texture is generous and mouth filling, while the acid cuts through, vibrant, clean, and zesty. This is a great partner for slightly spicy Asian dishes featuring vegetables, chicken, pork, and seafood.

NOTES

....
....
....
....

GREECE

GREECE DOESN'T FEATURE PROMINENTLY on many people's wine radars (until they visit the country), but it produces a lot of good-value wine. Although international grape varieties are becoming more popular there, it's good to see that many wines are still made using indigenous varieties.

Wines labelled PGI followed by a region are regional wines made from varieties approved for that region.

★ ★ ★ ★   **Boutari Moschofilero 2014**

PGI MANTINIA $13.10 (172387) 11% ALC.   **D**

Moschofilero is a grape variety indigenous to Greece that produces
aromatic wines with good acidity. This is true to type, and it's an excellent
choice for roast chicken and pork and for spicy (think Asian) dishes of
many kinds. The flavours are rich in spicy fruitiness and hold on right
through the palate, and the acidity comes though clean and refreshing. It's
definitely worth trying.

NOTES
....
....
....
....

★ ★ ★ ★ ★   **Troupis 'FTERI' Moscholfilero 2013**

PGI ARCADIA $15.60 (392936) 12% ALC.   **XD**

This is a lovely dry white made from the moschofilero variety. There are
delicate hints of muscat on the nose and some light fruitiness on the
palate, but it's above all well structured and complex, with an excellent
balance between the fruit and the bright, clean acid. You can enjoy this
with poultry, pork, white fish, and seafood, but it will extend to spicy
Asian-inspired dishes too.

NOTES
....
....
....
....

HUNGARY

HUNGARY HAS A WINE HISTORY that goes back two thousand years, and the country is best known for its sweet wine from the Tokaji district. There are many Hungarian dry wines, and although they have made little impact on the Canadian market, they are becoming more widely available. One of Hungary's best white grape varieties is hárslevelü, but many other varieties are grown.

Debrői Hárslevelü 2014

★ ★ ★ ★

AOP VDDETTE EREDETD $8.50 (536268) 12.5% ALC. **M**
KLASSZIKUS BOR

Made from Hungary's signature white grape variety, hárslevelü, this
is fairly sweet and fruity and shows a nice clean and crisp acidity that
balances the sweetness effectively. It's a lighter white that makes a good
choice with spicy seafood, chicken, and white fish, as well as many lighter
Asian dishes.

NOTES

....

....

....

....

ITALY

ITALY, THE SECOND LARGEST wine-producer in the world, has a long history of producing white wines from indigenous grapes, but in recent years we've seen increasing numbers made from international varieties, such as chardonnay. One international grape grown in many Italian regions is pinot grigio (also known as pinot gris). There are many mediocre pinot grigios, but this list identifies a number that stand out from the herd for quality and value.

The highest-quality classification of Italian wines is DOCG *(Denominazione di Origine Controllata e Garantita),* which indicates a wine made to stringent regulations and from a few specified grape varieties. Wines in the next category, DOC *(Denominazione di Origine Controllata),* follow similar rules. Wines labelled IGT *(Indicazione Geografica Tipica)* or IGP *(Indicazione Geografica Protetta)* are made according to less-stringent regulations and may use a wider range of grape varieties. This doesn't mean that a DOCG or DOC wine is necessarily better than an IGT/IGP—in fact, some of Italy's most famous (and expensive) wines are classified IGT/IGP. Overall, you'll find quality and value in all these categories, as this list shows.

★★★★ ½ **Anselmi San Vincenzo 2014**

IGT VENETO $16.70 (948158) 12.7% ALC.   D

[Vintages Essential] From northeastern Italy, this is a blend of an Italian grape, garganega, and two international varieties, chardonnay and sauvignon blanc. It's a ménage à trois that really works. Look for sweet fruit in this dry wine, finely balanced by bright, crisp acidity. It's a great wine for summer sipping or as an aperitif, and it goes well with many seafood, fish, and poultry dishes.

NOTES
....
....
....
....

NEW!
★★★★ **Bolla Soave Classico 2014**

DOC SOAVE CLASSICO $10.95 (438945) 12.7% ALC.   XD

"Soave" means "soft" in Italian, and that's one way of describing the texture of this wine. At the same time, it has the bright and breezy acidity to make it refreshing and a very successful partner with food. Pair it with dishes that are subtle rather than assertive: simple seafood, white fish, and poultry. The flavours are quite complex, and they range from herbs to sweet fruits.

NOTES
....
....
....
....

★★★★★ **Bollini Pinot Grigio 2014**

DOC TRENTINO $16.95 (951319) 13% ALC.   XD

There's a lot going on in a glass of this wine—far more than in too many pinot grigios on the market. The fruit is luscious and generous, but also well structured and complex, with many dimensions in the flavour profile. The acidity is perfectly calibrated to the fruit, giving fresh juiciness to the texture. This is a great pairing with well-seasoned roast pork or chicken, and will easily extend to seafood and to moderately spicy dishes.

NOTES
....
....
....
....

Cavallina Grillo/Pinot Grigio 2014

★ ★ ★ ★ ½

IGP TERRE SICILIANE $8.80 (123166) 12% ALC.   D

Grillo is a grape variety widely planted in Sicily, where it can withstand high temperatures. It produces high acidity that translates as a zesty, vibrant texture, the sort you see here. Blended with pinot grigio, which gives a lot of fruit flavour, it makes an easy-drinking white on its own, or pairs well with spicy dishes and many ways of preparing chicken, white fish, shellfish, and seafood.

NOTES

....

....

....

....

Citra Trebbiano d'Abruzzo 2015

★ ★ ★ ★

DOC TREBBIANO D'ABRUZZO $8.35 (522144) 12% ALC.   XD

Like many Italian wine names, this one combines a grape variety (trebbiano) and a region (Abruzzo). It's medium bodied and has an attractively dry feel. Look for very pleasant and fairly complex fruit flavours and a clean and refreshing texture that makes for a good match with creamy Italian dishes. Try it with fettuccine alfredo or any pasta prepared in a cream sauce. It's also available in a 1.5 L bottle.

NOTES

....

....

....

....

Danzante Pinot Grigio 2014

★ ★ ★ ★ ½

IGT DELLE VENEZIE $15.10 (26906) 12% ALC.   XD

"Dance the pure emotion of Italian wine," the label urges. Well, the texture in this pinot grigio is lively and refreshing and it's in step with the flavours, which are nicely paced, quite complex, and concentrated. Neither leads—they dance side-by-side. If you want to add another partner (this could get complicated), try grilled white fish, herbed roast chicken, or grilled garlic shrimp.

NOTES

....

....

....

....

Fazi Battaglia Verdicchio dei Castelli di Jesi Classico 2014

★ ★ ★ ★

DOC VERDICCHIO DEI CASTELLI $9.60 (24422) 12% ALC.   XD
DI JESI CLASSICO

Fazi Battaglia packages its verdicchio in a distinctive bottle that looks a bit like an elongated, green Coca-Cola bottle. But the contents are much, much better! There are lovely understated but positive fruit flavours and a touch of tanginess for good measure. With its very good fruit-acid balance and crisp texture, this wine is ideal for many seafood and white fish dishes.

NOTES

....

....

....

....

Gabbiano 'Promessa' Pinot Grigio 2014

★ ★ ★ ★ ½

IGT DELLE VENEZIE $13.10 (77990) 12% ALC.   XD

The Castello di Gabbiano, home of this winery, is a 13th-century castle in Tuscany that is now also an elegant hotel. This pinot grigio from the Venice region is equally elegant. It shows lovely flavours that are fresh and substantial and a texture that's round, smooth, and very refreshing. Dry and medium bodied, it's a wine you can sip as an aperitif or drink with rich or slightly spicy seafood, chicken, turkey, or pork.

NOTES

....

....

....

....

Masi Masianco 2014

★ ★ ★ ★ ½

IGT VENEZIE $16.65 (620773) 13% ALC.   D

This is a very attractive blend of pinot grigio and verduzzo, with the verduzzo having been dried before being pressed to increase the intensity and complexity. The result is a white with real depth, while the pinot grigio contributes fresh fruitiness. Dry and medium weight, it's refreshing on its own or excellent paired with poultry, white fish, seafood, and pork.

NOTES

....

....

....

....

Masi Modello delle Venezie 2014

★ ★ ★ ★

IGT BIANCO DELLE VENEZIE $12.10 (564674) 12% ALC.   D

Made predominantly with pinot grigio, ably assisted by some indigenous varieties, this is a straightforward, easy-drinking, and fruity white that's nicely balanced to ensure a clean and crisp texture. This stands very well on its own, and it's quite versatile with food. Try it with spicy Asian dishes, roast chicken or pork, or with creamy pastas.

NOTES

....

....

....

....

....

Ruffino 'Lumina' Pinot Grigio 2013

★ ★ ★ ★ ½

IGT DELLE VENEZIE $13.45 (589101) 12% ALC.   D

This is quite an elegant pinot grigio for the price. The texture is smooth and mouth-filling, but it retains freshness from the broad seam of acidity, and the flavours are well defined and focused. It's dry and medium bodied and goes well with chicken, pork, and mild cheeses.

NOTES

....

....

....

....

....

Ruffino Orvieto Classico 2014

★ ★ ★ ★

DOC ORVIETO CLASSICO $12.95 (31062) 12% ALC.   D

From vineyards near the beautiful town of Orvieto (the cathedral is shown on the label), this is a versatile dry white that's easy drinking on its own and a good match for lighter chicken, seafood and fish dishes, as well as for summer salads. The flavours show pure fruit, the acidity is refreshing and the balance very good.

NOTES

....

....

....

....

....

NEW ZEALAND

NEW ZEALAND IS A VERY SMALL PRODUCER of wine in global terms, but it made a big name for itself in the wine world in the 1990s with sauvignon blancs, especially those from Marlborough. They're still the core of the country's white wines, but chardonnay and other white varieties (and other regions) are definitely worth trying.

Alpine Valley Sauvignon Blanc 2015

★ ★ ★ ★

MARLBOROUGH $15.10 (241810) 13% ALC. **XD**

The Marlborough wine region, New Zealand's biggest, lies in the South Island at the northern end of the Southern Alps, a snow-capped range that runs all the way to the Central Otago wine region. This "savvy" (as it's called in New Zealand) is bright and fresh, with quite dense and pungent flavours and a juicy texture. It's a good choice for oysters, seafood, and white fish.

NOTES

....

....

....

....

Astrolabe Sauvignon Blanc 2015

★ ★ ★ ★ ½

MARLBOROUGH $22.95 (10421) 13% ALC. **D**

[Vintages Essential] The vibrant acidity is the first component to strike you when you taste this sauvignon and the clean, fresh flavours follow quickly. They're very well balanced, and this is a less intense sauvignon than many others from Marlborough. That makes it more suitable for many foods, and I'd be very happy with a glass of this and a dozen oysters, or grilled white fish or shrimps.

NOTES

....

....

....

....

Babich Sauvignon Blanc 2015

★ ★ ★ ★ ½

MARLBOROUGH $16.15 (620054) 13% ALC. **XD**

The Babich family first cultivated vines early in the 20th century near Auckland, but the grapes for this wine come from much farther south, in the famed Marlborough region. This gives the wine its classic New Zealand sauvignon blanc flavours of exciting and pungent fruit. It's crisp and refreshing with a smooth texture, and it goes wonderfully with a warm goat cheese salad or tomato and goat cheese quiche.

NOTES

....

....

....

....

Brancott 'B' Sauvignon Blanc 2013
★ ★ ★ ★ ★
MARLBOROUGH $19.95 (278689) 14% ALC. D

Here's a luscious sauvignon blanc from Marlborough, offering that great one-two combination of ripe and complex fruit flavours and refreshing, assertive acidity that makes you whimper for a plate of oysters or white fish irrigated with lemon juice. Some of Marlborough sauvignons are a bit over the top in flavour intensity and acidity, but this one keeps everything in the right place.

NOTES
....
....
....
....

NEW!
★ ★ ★ ★ ★
Cloudy Bay Sauvignon Blanc 2015
MARLBOROUGH $33.95 (304469) 13.5% ALC. XD

[Vintages Essential] Cloudy Bay did more than any other brand to put Marlborough sauvignon blanc on the world wine map. The style has evolved but it's no less a fine wine now than in the 1990s. Look for elegant flavours that are bright and serious, focused and well defined, and supported by brisk, clean acidity. It captures a style less assertive than many Marlborough sauvignons, and it's an excellent choice for briny oysters and many other seafoods.

NOTES
....
....
....
....

Kim Crawford Sauvignon Blanc 2015
★ ★ ★ ★ ½
MARLBOROUGH $19.95 (35386) 13.5% ALC. XD

[Vintages Essential] This is an elegant sauvignon blanc that delivers lovely, well-structured flavours right through the palate. They're fresh and broad, with plenty of complexity, and they're supported by crisp, clean acidity that gives the wine its notable food friendliness. This is a terrific choice for freshly shucked oysters with lemon, as it is with many other white fish and seafoods.

NOTES
....
....

NEW!
★★★★

Kim Crawford Unoaked Chardonnay 2014

EAST COAST $19.95 (991950) 14% ALC.   XD

Parts of the east coast of the North Island of New Zealand (regions like
Hawkes Bay and Gisborne) capture lots of sunshine ad produce lovely
wines. This chardonnay is full of fresh fruit flavours that are vibrant and
appealing, and they're supported by the same kind of acidity. Together
they make for an excellent partnership with poultry, seafood, white fish,
and mild-flavoured cheeses.

NOTES

★★★★★

Matua Sauvignon Blanc 2015

HAWKES BAY $17.15 (619452) 13% ALC.   XD

If you're feeling a little jaded from your diet of Marlborough sauvignon
blanc, try this one from Hawkes Bay, a region on the east coast of New
Zealand's North Island. It's a little different, a little fruitier, but it has the
same style of plush and well-focused fruit flavours together with a full and
refreshing texture. This is a great choice for grilled white fish or seafood,
but try it with mussels steamed in white wine and garlic too.

NOTES

★★★★ ½

Oyster Bay Chardonnay 2014

MARLBOROUGH $18.95 (326728) 13.7% ALC.   XD

[Vintages Essential] This is an elegant chardonnay that shows the
lightest touch of oak, a mere hint of toastiness in the concentrated, well-
calibrated, and delicious flavours. The acidity checks in softly but is
remarkably effective, adding freshness and vibrancy to the fruit. This is
an excellent choice for roast chicken and pork, but it will also work with
white fish and seafood.

NOTES

Oyster Bay Sauvignon Blanc 2015

★ ★ ★ ★ ½

MARLBOROUGH $18.95 (316570) 11% ALC. **XD**

[Vintages Essential] Here's a well-named wine. One of the classic food pairings with sauvignon blanc is freshly shucked oysters. The richness and acidity of the wine pick up the texture and brininess of the shellfish. This sauvignon is quite lovely, with concentrated and pungent flavours that flow in on a tide that's crisp and refreshing. If you don't have fresh oysters on hand, try grilled white fish with fresh lemon.

NOTES

Peter Yealands Sauvignon Blanc 2014

★ ★ ★ ★ ★

MARLBOROUGH $16.10 (277731) 13% ALC. **XD**

This is a very attractive sauvignon that combines fruit concentration with a lightness that suits it well to food—there's no threat of heavy, pungent fruit overpowering your white fish, shellfish, or poultry. Look for good complexity and balance through and through, with bright acidity coming through as juiciness on the palate. It's a well-made wine that's eminently food friendly and versatile.

NOTES

Riverlore Sauvignon Blanc 2015

★ ★ ★ ★

MARLBOROUGH $15.95 (417600) 13% ALC. **XD**

The label shows a taniwha, a being in Maori mythology that inhabits dangerous waters. But there are no dangerous waters here. Instead you'll find a well-paced sauvignon with bright fruit and a good acid balance, although the acidity is softer and less assertive than in many Marlborough sauvignons. This is an easy-going sipping wine that also pairs with poultry and pork dishes, though it lacks the acidity for oysters and lemon-drizzled fish or seafood.

NOTES

Saint Clair Sauvignon Blanc 2014

★ ★ ★ ★

MARLBOROUGH $17.15 (237255) 13% ALC. **XD**

This is a sauvignon blanc you can serve with a variety of foods, from freshly shucked oysters to fish and chips, from roast chicken to moderately hot curries. It shows bright fruit from start to finish, with decent complexity and good focus. The acidity shines through clear, clean, and crisp, and all the components are nicely integrated.

NOTES
....
....
....
....

Stoneleigh Sauvignon Blanc 2015

★ ★ ★ ★

MARLBOROUGH $17.95 (293043) 13% ALC. **XD**

Marlborough gets more sunshine each year than almost any other part of New Zealand. Combine that with cool temperatures and you have perfect conditions for sauvignon blancs like this one. The fruit is ripe, sweet, and pungent, and it's undergirded with vibrant acidity. The result is a mouth-watering wine that sets you up for food. Seafood, shellfish, and white fish are the classics, but try it with curried dishes too.

NOTES
....
....
....
....

Villa Maria 'Private Bin' Sauvignon Blanc 2015

★ ★ ★ ★ ½

MARLBOROUGH $17.45 (426601) 13% ALC. **XD**

Villa Maria is a well-established New Zealand winery that I used to visit when I was a teenager living in Auckland. It's now transformed from a small local producer to a global exporter, thanks to wines like this sauvignon blanc. It delivers concentrated and well-defined flavours and a vibrant texture that picks up the natural acidity of the grape variety. It's an ideal choice for grilled white fish with a squeeze of lemon.

NOTES
....
....
....
....

★ ★ ★ ★

White Cliff 'Winemaker's Selection' Sauvignon Blanc 2015

MARLBOROUGH $14.95 (610972) 12.5% ALC. **XD**

This is a sauvignon blanc made in the classic Marlborough style that first put New Zealand on the world wine map. The flavours are rich, pungent, complex, and well defined, and there's a terrific seam of acidity running right through, contributing a clean, bright, zesty texture. It goes well with oysters and other seafood, white fish, or a tomato and goat cheese tart.

NOTES
....
....
....
....

★ ★ ★ ★ ½

Whitehaven Sauvignon Blanc 2015

MARLBOROUGH $19.15 (308288) 13% ALC. **D**

This has the rich complexity of many Marlborough sauvignons, but in this one the flavours are extraordinarily pure, well defined, and nicely focused. They flow through the palate on a stream of bright, zesty acidity, and the flavours stay with you through the finish. It's a great choice for oysters and other white fish and seafood, especially with a drizzle of lemon juice.

NOTES
....
....
....
....

ONTARIO

SOME OF THE BEST WINES produced in Ontario are white. The cool growing conditions allow the grapes to ripen while achieving the levels of acidity they need to be crisp and refreshing. The most successful white varieties in the province are riesling, chardonnay, sauvignon blanc, and gewürztraminer.

VQA (Vintners Quality Alliance) on an Ontario wine label, followed by the name of a wine region, means that the wine was made from grapes grown in that region and that the wine was tested and tasted for quality. Wines labelled VQA with an Ontario region can be made only from grapes grown in Ontario. The designated wine regions are Niagara Peninsula (and its sub-regions, such as Beamsville Bench and Niagara-on-the-Lake), Lake Erie North Shore, and Prince Edward County. Wines labelled VQA Ontario are made from grapes grown in any region.

Bachelder Chardonnay 2013

★ ★ ★ ★ ★

VQA NIAGARA PENINSULA $24.95 (302083) 13% ALC   XD

[Vintages Essential] This reasonably full-bodied chardonnay delivers intense and well-focused flavours that persist right through the palate. The acidity clicks in on the attack and carries the fruit with juicy freshness, setting the wine up for food. This is a white for weightier dishes, and it goes well with well-seasoned pork and chicken, as well as with richer seafoods such as lobster and scallops.

NOTES

....

....

....

....

Cave Spring Chardonnay 2014

★ ★ ★ ★

VQA NIAGARA ESCARPMENT $15.95 (228551) 13% ALC. XD

Wine writers occasionally refer to the ABC movement, meaning Anything But Chardonnay, because, supposedly, many people are tired of chardonnay. This example might well change their minds. For the price, it's quite rich and stylish, with solid, mouth-filling fruit flavours, and it has a very crisp, juicy texture. You'll enjoy this with lobster or with rich turkey, chicken, and pork dishes.

NOTES

....

....

....

....

Cave Spring Dry Riesling 2014

★ ★ ★ ★ ½

VQA NIAGARA PENINSULA $15.95 (233635) 11.5% ALC. D

Cave Spring quickly established a reputation for riesling, and it's still among the best producers of the variety in Ontario. Its rieslings tend to be stylish and complex, and they go beautifully with food. This one has a very crisp, clean, and generous texture that's complemented by lovely nuanced fruit flavours. It's dry, refreshing, and medium bodied. You can sip it as an aperitif, but it has the stuff to go with smoked chicken or pork tenderloin.

NOTES

....

....

....

Cave Spring 'Estate Bottled' Riesling 2014

★ ★ ★ ★ ★

VQA BEAMSVILLE BENCH $18.95 (286377) 12% ALC.   D

[Vintages Essential] Beamsville Bench is one of more than a dozen sub-appellations (or sub-regions) of the Niagara Peninsula appellation (wine region). It might be a bit confusing for consumers, but what's *not* confusing is this only-just-off-dry riesling. It delivers delicious, intense flavours on a texture that's brisk, fresh, and clean, and it sets you up for food. So eat. Drink this with spicy seafood or smoked salmon.

NOTES

....
....
....
....

Cave Spring Riesling 2014

★ ★ ★ ★ ½

VQA NIAGARA PENINSULA $15.95 (234583) 11% ALC.   D

This is a gorgeous off-dry example of riesling that displays rich, luscious, well-nuanced fruit flavours accompanied by a texture that's plush and mouth-filling but also zesty and refreshing. It's the perfect wine for slightly spicy seafood, chicken, and pork dishes, or for Thai or Indian food, whether vegetarian or meat-based.

NOTES

....
....
....
....

Cave Spring Sauvignon Blanc 2014

★ ★ ★ ★

VQA NIAGARA ESCARPMENT $16.95 (529933) 13% ALC. XD

This is a lovely sauvignon blanc that goes well with grilled white fish with a squeeze of lemon, freshly shucked oysters, or fish and chips (but avoid vinegar and stick to lemon). Made in a classic and popular style, this sauvignon blanc is dry and medium bodied, with a crisp, refreshing texture that lifts and enhances the well-defined yet quite restrained flavours.

NOTES

....
....
....
....

Château des Charmes Aligoté 2015

★ ★ ★ ★ ½

VQA ST. DAVID'S BENCH $14.95 (296848) 13% ALC.   **D**

Aligoté is a little-known variety from Burgundy, where most of the white wine is made from chardonnay. This Ontario aligoté has the crisp texture and clean and refreshing aftertaste that's characteristic of the variety, making it ideal for shellfish. It has rich and concentrated flavours and a fairly round mouth feel. Try it with roast chicken or grilled pork chops, too.

NOTES

....

....

....

....

Château des Charmes 'Barrel Fermented' Chardonnay 2014

★ ★ ★ ★ ★

VQA NIAGARA-ON-THE-LAKE $14.95 (81653) 12% ALC.   **XD**

This is an especially delicious chardonnay in a style that I find irresistible because it seamlessly combines weight and elegance. Look for plush and well-defined fruit that's nicely complex with a round, smooth, mouth-filling and very refreshing texture. The oak is exceptionally well managed and enhances the flavours and texture. The wine is very well balanced and is an excellent choice for poultry, pork, and even rich dishes like lobster and seared scallops.

NOTES

....

....

....

....

Château des Charmes Sauvignon Blanc 2015

★ ★ ★ ★ ½

VQA ST. DAVID'S BENCH $14.95 (391300) 12.5% ALC.   **XD**

St. David's Bench is a sub-appellation within the Niagara Peninsula wine region. This sauvignon blanc is really lovely, with lively, bright, but also solid and substantial flavours. Thanks to quite vibrant acidity, the texture is rich, refreshing, and lively. This is a dry and medium-bodied wine that's excellent with grilled white fish (or fish and chips) and freshly squeezed lemon.

NOTES

....

....

....

Coyote's Run 'Five Mile' White 2014

★ ★ ★ ★

VQA NIAGARA PENINSULA $14.95 (195669) 11.5% ALC.   D

This is a blend of riesling, pinot gris, and chardonnay, all grape varieties that do well in Ontario. It's off-dry, with bright and somewhat pungent flavours allied with a broad seam of fresh, vibrant acidity. It's the style of wine that's frequently suggested for spicy food, and this one goes well with sushi and many dishes in the Thai culinary tradition.

NOTES

Coyote's Run Pinot Grigio 2015

NEW!
★ ★ ★ ★

VQA NIAGARA PENINSULA $15.95 (112144) 12% ALC.   D

This is a very successful pinot grigio that delivers attractive, bright flavours that are persistent right through the palate. The supporting acidity is very well balanced, making this a versatile wine at the table. Pair it with chicken, pork, seafood, or white fish, or with many lightly spicy Asian dishes. Or you can drink it on its own.

NOTES

Creekside Pinot Grigio 2014

★ ★ ★ ★ ½

VQA NIAGARA PENINSULA $14.95 (83196) 12.2% ALC.   XD

This is a very attractive pinot grigio with well-defined and complex flavours and a great clean, crisp, refreshing texture. There's a pink tinge to the wine from the grape skins, which are often a greyish-pink colour. It's not as fruity as many pinot grigios, and the texture makes it an excellent choice for many foods. Try it with chicken, pork, or shellfish (such as mussels steamed in white wine).

NOTES

Creekside Sauvignon Blanc 2014

★★★★ ½

VQA NIAGARA PENINSULA $14.95 (620724) 12.7% ALC.   **XD**

This is a vibrant, crisp sauvignon with persistent fresh and nicely complex flavours. The acidity plays a great role here and contributes to making the wine versatile at the table. Drink it with the usual sauvignon suspects (oysters, seafood, white fish, goat cheese) but you can also try it with medium-hot curries or fish and chips.

NOTES

....

....

....

....

....

Fielding 'Fireside' White 2014

★★★★ ½

VQA NIAGARA PENINSULA $13.95 (303040) 11% ALC.   **M**

A very attractive blend of riesling, gewürzrtraminer, and chardonnay musqué, this wine shows both complexity and vibrancy. The tension is evident in the flavours—which are complex and sweet-centred—and the full (but clean and crisp) texture. The gewürztraminer and chardonnay musqué push towards spicy dishes, and the riesling towards roast chicken and grilled fish. They all pair with the one wine.

NOTES

....

....

....

....

Fielding Pinot Gris 2013

★★★★

VQA NIAGARA PENINSULA $16.95 (223610) 12.5% ALC.   **D**

There's a little sweetness here, but don't avoid this if your preference is for dry wines. The flavour complexity and well-calibrated acidity give the wine a dry feel, and it ends quite astringently. Medium bodied and quite elegant, this is a great choice for spicy seafood, shellfish, or poultry dishes, whether or not they're Asian-inspired.

NOTES

....

....

....

....

★ ★ ★ ★ **Fielding Estate Riesling 2014**

VQA NIAGARA PENINSULA $15.95 (146761) 10.5% ALC. **M**

Fielding's logo is a Muskoka chair, and this is the kind of wine you want when you kick back to relax. It's off-dry with a good dose of acidity to keep the sweetness under control, and it has a crisp, clean feel in your mouth. Sip it on its own, serve it as an aperitif, or drink it with spicy Asian dishes or with melon and prosciutto.

NOTES
....
....
....
....
....

★ ★ ★ ★ ½ **Flat Rock 'Good Kharma' Chardonnay 2014**

VQA NIAGARA PENINSULA $17.15 (356873) 13.4% ALC. **XD**

This is a rich chardonnay that shows plush, round fruit from start to finish. But—and this is important—the opulence of the fruit is very effectively balanced by a broad seam of clean, fresh acidity. It sets the wine up perfectly for fairly rich pork and poultry dishes. Why "Good Kharma"? Some of the proceeds from sales go to the Ontario Association of Food Banks.

NOTES
....
....
....
....

★ ★ ★ ★ ½ **Flat Rock Twisted 2014**

VQA NIAGARA PENINSULA $17.15 (1578) 12% ALC. **M**

[Vintages Essential] This blend of riesling, gewürztraminer, and chardonnay is drier that most similar combinations, thanks to the fresh acidity that underlies the fruit. The flavours are generous but nicely nuanced and focused, and the texture is crisp and clean. It's a natural for many Asian dishes with sweet spices, and goes well with many pork and chicken dishes too.

NOTES
....
....
....
....

Grange of Prince Edward County Pinot Gris 2014

NEW!
★ ★ ★ ★ ½

VQA PRINCE EDWARD COUNTY $17.15 (69336) 12% ALC.   XD

This is a very well-made 100 percent pinot gris that you can enjoy on its own or pair with a wide range of dishes such as poultry, pork, seafood, and mildly spicy dishes of many kinds. It shows ripe-sweet aromas and flavours that are consistent right through the palate as well as an impressively balanced seam of clean, bright acidity. Overall, it's well integrated and a pleasure to drink.

NOTES
....
....
....
....

Guilty Men White 2014

★ ★ ★ ★ ½

VQA NIAGARA PENINSULA $14.95 (192666) 12.5% ALC.   D

There's something about "guilty men" and the 666 in the product code. Made by the always-reliable Malivoire winery, this blend of riesling and sauvignon blanc is wicked with food. It's crisp and bright and essentially dry, but there's a nuance of fruit sweetness that lets you pair it with spicier foods (think Thai). It also pairs well with roast chicken, pork, and grilled white fish and seafood. All in all, one of those guilty pleasures.

NOTES
....
....
....
....

Henry of Pelham Chardonnay 2014

★ ★ ★ ★ ½

VQA NIAGARA PENINSULA $14.95 (291211) 13% ALC.   XD

This wine was made and aged in stainless steel to preserve the purity of the fruit flavours. It worked. This is just a very well-made wine—nothing to make you run screaming into the street, but a wine to enjoy. The sweet and ripe flavours are substantial but nuanced and delicate, and the texture is clean and refreshing. It's a natural for roast chicken or pork as well as for simply prepared white fish.

NOTES
....
....
....
....

★ ★ ★ ★ ½ Henry of Pelham Riesling 2015

VQA NIAGARA PENINSULA $14.95 (268375) 10.5% ALC.   D

Riesling has led the way with screw caps—first in New Zealand and Australia, then elsewhere. The seal captures the freshness you want in the variety, and Henry of Pelham delivers with this example. It's a dry riesling packed with delicious flavours and a round and crisp, clean texture. It's a great choice for sipping on the deck or before dinner, but it's also excellent with fish, seafood, chicken, or pork dishes.

NOTES
....
....
....
....

★ ★ ★ ★ Henry of Pelham Sauvignon Blanc 2014

VQA NIAGARA PENINSULA $14.95 (430546) 12.5% ALC.   XD

This very attractive sauvignon blanc has all the zesty crispness of texture and brightness of fruit you look for in this variety, without the pungency that often overpowers food. The flavours are lively and textured, it's dry and medium bodied, and it goes well with shellfish, seafood, or grilled or pan-fried white fish with fresh lemon.

NOTES
....
....
....
....

★ ★ ★ ★ ★ Kacaba Unoaked Chardonnay 2014

VQA NIAGARA PENINSULA $14.95 (326975) 13.5% ALC.   XD

This is a clean, crisp chardonnay that delivers very attractive flavours and makes a versatile white for the table. The fruit is ripe-sweet at the core, with good complexity, and the acidity is fresh and vibrant, adding a lovely juiciness to the texture. It's dry and harmonious, and makes a very good partner for many poultry, pork, and white fish dishes.

NOTES
....
....
....
....

Malivoire Chardonnay 2014

★ ★ ★ ★ ½

VQA BEAMSVILLE BENCH $19.95 (573147) 13.2% ALC.   **XD**

[Vintages Essential] This well-crafted chardonnay is a great choice for richer dishes (made richer by seasonings, sauces, or condiments) featuring chicken and pork, but will easily extend to grilled salmon and richer seafood like lobster and scallops. The fruit is plush, complex, and persistent, with hints of sweet oak, and the acidity is clean and refreshing.

NOTES

....

....

....

....

....

Megalomaniac 'Homegrown Cellar 4379' Riesling 2013

★ ★ ★ ★

VQA NIAGARA PENINSULA $14.95 (183061) 10.5% ALC.   **MS**

This is a sweeter riesling but the acidity kicks in to moderate the residual sugar. You end up with a wine you can chill down and drink on its own, or that you can pair with many spicy pork, chicken, tofu, or vegetarian dishes. The flavours are solid right through the palate, and they're bright and fruity, while the acidity is clean and refreshing and well calibrated to the intensity of the fruit.

NOTES

....

....

....

....

Megalomaniac 'Narcissist' Riesling 2013

★ ★ ★ ★ ★

VQA NIAGARA PENINSULA $17.95 (67587) 10.9% ALC.   **D**

[Vintages Essential] This is a lovely off-dry riesling with a racy, juicy texture that makes you think of food. The flavours are rich and well-sculpted, and the acidity takes care of much of the sweetness. This is a riesling that can swing dry and off-dry. Enjoy it with the spicy dishes that off-dries often call for, but don't hesitate to pour it with rich chicken and pork dishes too.

NOTES

....

....

....

....

Peninsula Ridge 'Inox' Unoaked Chardonnay 2014

★ ★ ★ ★ ½

VQA NIAGARA PENINSULA $14.95 (594200) 12.5% ALC. **XD**

No oak barrels were harmed in the making of this chardonnay. Inox refers to the stainless steel tanks that the wine is made in, and the purpose of using stainless steel is to present the fruit flavours and texture without any oak influence. What you get here are beautifully clean, pure flavours and excellent balance. It's almost full bodied, with a generous texture, and pairs well with pork, chicken, and white fish.

NOTES

Peninsula Ridge Sauvignon Blanc 2014

★ ★ ★ ★ ½

VQA NIAGARA PENINSULA $14.95 (53678) 13.3% ALC. **XD**

Peninsula Ridge was the first winery where I tasted an Ontario sauvignon blanc I thought was stunning. It's vintage variable, but this one is full of sauvignon character, with vibrant and pungent fruit flavours, a mouth-filling texture that's high in bright, refreshing acidity, and a long, clean finish. Drink it with the usual suspects—freshly shucked oysters—or with battered white fish, chips, and tartar sauce.

NOTES

Southbrook 'Connect' Organic White 2015

★ ★ ★ ★ ½

VQA ONTARIO $15.95 (249078) 9.6% ALC. **D**

This attractive and fruity blend of vidal, riesling, and sauvignon blanc has plenty of flavour, good focus and intensity, and the acidity to give it a bright and crisp texture. It's easy drinking in the best sense of the phrase, and you can enjoy it on its own or pair it with sushi and other spicy Asian dishes.

NOTES

NEW!
★ ★ ★ ★ ★

Sprucewood Shores Riesling 2014

VQA ONTARIO $13.95 (326249) 12.5% ALC.   **M**

This is a lovely, slightly more than off-dry riesling that goes very well with spicy dishes, whether in the broad Asian tradition or not. Enjoy it with curries, pad Thais, and medium-spiced Chinese dishes, for example. The flavours are quite luscious, with plenty of complexity, and the acidity is bright and balanced. The fruit and acid are balanced very well.

NOTES
....
....
....
....

NEW!
★ ★ ★ ★ ★

Tawse 'Quarry Road' Riesling 2014

VQA VINEMOUNT RIDGE $24.25 (198853) 10% ALC.   **M**

[Vintages Essential] Many people shy away from wines that don't seem to be dry, but then love somewhat sweeter wines when they try them. The secret is the balance, as this terrific riesling shows by balancing the sweetness and acidity, where the acidity cuts through the sugar and renders the flavours more fruity than sweet. This is a great wine to sip on its own or to pair with spicy Asian cuisine or well-seasoned pork and poultry dishes.

NOTES
....
....
....
....

NEW!
★ ★ ★ ★

Tawse 'Sketches of Niagara' Chardonnay 2013

VQA NIAGARA PENINSULA $21.95 (89037) 13% ALC.   **XD**

[Vintages Essential] This is a terrific chardonnay from one of Niagara's highly regarded producers. Look for real purity in the fruit, which is full of well-defined, nicely focused, and ripe flavours. They're backed by clean and fresh acidity that contributes food-friendly juiciness to the texture. This wine goes very well with many pork and poultry dishes.

NOTES
....
....
....
....
....

PORTUGAL

PORTUGAL DOESN'T SHOW VERY brightly on the radar of Ontario wine drinkers, and when it does, it's more for the reds than the whites. The best-known Portuguese white wine is vinho verde, a fruity and slightly spritzy wine that's meant to be drunk young and cold, but there are other interesting whites made from indigenous grapes.

Portugal's official wine regions are indicated by DOC *(Denominação de Origem Controlada)* on the label. Others are labelled as regional wines *(Vinho Regional).*

Quinta da Aveleda Vinho Verde 2014

★ ★ ★ ★

DOC VINHO VERDE $10.45 (5322) 9.5% ALC.   D

I can see sipping this before a meal throughout the year, or while sitting
on a deck or lounging at the cottage in the summer. It's a simple, light
white with a low alcohol level of 9.5 percent (just what you need in the
summer), sweet fruit flavours, and a light spritziness that adds to its
refreshing, palate-cleansing character. You can also enjoy it with spicy
appetizers.

NOTES

....

....

....

....

SOUTH AFRICA

SOUTH AFRICA'S WINE REGIONS are mostly warm, which makes you think red wine. But they produce many very good–quality whites, too. The most popular variety used to be chenin blanc, but over the last ten years others (especially chardonnay and sauvignon blanc) have become more important.

Wines from official South African wine regions are called Wines of Origin. The letters WO, followed by a region, indicate where the wine is from.

★ ★ ★ ★
The Beachhouse Sauvignon Blanc 2015
WO WESTERN CAPE $10.05 (122390) 13% ALC. D

This a well-made, easy-drinking sauvignon that shows all the solid, bright flavours and crispness you look for in sauvignon blanc. It doesn't have the weight and power of most Marlborough sauvignons, and you can enjoy it on its own. It also goes well with many seafood and white fish dishes, as well as not-too-hot curries and Asian dishes.

NOTES
....
....
....
....
....

NEW!
★ ★ ★ ★
Fleur du Cap 'Bergkelder Selection' Chardonnay 2014
WO WESTERN CAPE $13.15 (358960) 14% ALC. XD

This is a lightly oaked chardonnay, where the oak has a subtle presence in the flavours and adds positively to the texture. The flavours are bright and ripe-sweet, and the clean and fresh acidity makes for a nice counterpoint. It's medium bodied and very well balanced. This is a very successful partner for grilled white fish, seafood, and medium-flavoured cheeses.

NOTES
....
....
....
....

★ ★ ★ ★ ★
Goats do Roam White 2014
WO COASTAL REGION $11.95 (237313) 13.5% ALC. XD

Not only does this winery have a herd of goats, the name is also a play on Côtes du Rhône, the French wine region. And, as it happens, this dry, medium-weight wine is made from grape varieties typical to that region: viognier (67 percent), roussanne (19 percent) and grenache blanc (14 percent). Look for great depth of flavour here, with good complexity and a refreshing and juicy texture. It's great with poultry, pork, and rich seafood dishes.

NOTES
....
....
....
....

Nederburg 'The Winemaster's Reserve' Sauvignon Blanc 2015
★ ★ ★ ★
WO WESTERN CAPE $12.10 (382713) 13% ALC. D

Nederburg is an established (over two centuries old) and big (production is about 13 million bottles a year) South African wine producer. Although, for wineries, age is sometimes seen as an advantage but size a problem, the company keeps quality up. This sauvignon blanc is zesty and refreshing, with good, clean flavours. It's made for food, so pair it with seafood or fish with a squeeze of lemon.

NOTES
....
....
....
....
....

The Wolftrap White 2014
★ ★ ★ ★ ★
WO FRANSCHHOEK $13.95 (292532) 13.5% ALC. XD

This terrific blend of viognier, chenin blanc, and grenache blanc is made by iconic producer Boekenhoutskloof. That's a mouthful, and so is this wine—a mouthful of plush, ripe-sweet fruit that's concentrated, layered, and consistent. It's supported by a broad seam of fresh acidity that gives it some juiciness. Drink it with pork or chicken, or with many spicy dishes.

NOTES
....
....
....
....
....

Two Oceans Sauvignon Blanc 2015
★ ★ ★ ★
WO WESTERN CAPE $9.95 (340380) 13% ALC. XD

This is a well-made, very drinkable sauvignon in a popular style. It's fruit-forward, not as assertive as, say, most Marlborough sauvignons, but it has more fruit definition than many Old World styles. Look for well-defined fruit, good concentration, crisp acidity, and then drink it with fish and chips (with lemon, not malt vinegar), seafood salads, and ceviche.

NOTES
....
....
....
....

SPAIN

SPAIN IS BEST KNOWN for its red wines, its sparkling wine, cava, and sherry. Much of the white table wine that Spain produces is consumed locally and never reaches international markets. However, that's changing as some of the larger wineries, like Torres, occasionally make white wines available in Vintages. Hopefully, some of these will eventually make their way to the LCBO.

The initials DO *(Denominación de Origen)* indicate a wine from one of Spain's designated wine regions. A higher-quality level, DOC *(Denominación de Origen Calificada),* has been awarded to only two regions, Rioja and Priorat.

Marqués de Riscal 2014
★ ★ ★ ★

DO RUEDA $12.55 (36822) 13% ALC.   **XD**

This is an attractive blend that's excellent for sipping on the patio or
before a meal. Serve it with grilled or pan-fried white fish or roast chicken.
It's dry and medium bodied, with attractive and fairly concentrated
fruit flavours. The texture is appealing, with richness from the fruit
complemented by a refreshing crispness that makes it great by itself or
with food.

NOTES
....
....
....
....

René Barbier Mediterranean White
★ ★ ★ ★

DO CATALUNYA $10.05 (332767) 12% ALC.   **XD**

[Non-vintage] This is a light-medium bodied white blend that's perfect for
sipping on its own—especially on a warm summer day. The fruit is fresh
and vibrant and the acidity is balanced, crisp, and clean. You can also
pair it with salads and with light, simple dishes featuring chicken, pork,
seafood, and white fish.

NOTES
....
....
....
....

Torres 'Viña Esmeralda' 2014
★ ★ ★ ★

DO CATALUNYA $13.95 (377465) 11.5% ALC.   **D**

Made from the muscat of Alexandria and gewürztaminer varieties, this is
a fruity, spicy, off-dry white that you can easily enjoy on its own or take
to the table, especially when you're eating Asian cuisine, spicy or well-
seasoned vegetables, poultry, or pork. It has a distinctly juicy texture,
thanks to the bright acidity that underlies the concentrated and consistent
fruit.

NOTES
....
....
....
....
....

WASHINGTON

THE STATE OF WASHINGTON is an important wine-producing region that's especially well known for merlots. Few Washington wines appear on LCBO shelves, but others are released from time to time by Vintages.

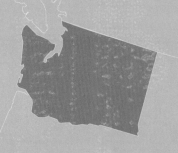

Charles & Charles Chardonnay 2014

★ ★ ★ ★

WASHINGTON $16.95 (394734) 13.8% ALC.   D

This is a very attractive chardonnay that's easy to drink on its own and can easily be paired with many pork and poultry dishes. Look for bright and nicely concentrated flavours from start to finish, and a good seam of vibrant acidity playing back-up. The balance is right and the texture is generous. It's just a good-value, nicely made chardonnay that holds together really well.

NOTES

....
....
....
....

Kung Fu Girl Riesling 2014

★ ★ ★ ★ ½

COLUMBIA VALLEY $19.15 (394759) 12% ALC.   M

This is an appealing riesling that lies in that food-versatile and deservedly popular space between dry and off-dry. That means you can serve it successfully with such dishes as unadorned roast chicken and smoked salmon, or pad Thai and well-seasoned grilled pork. The very attractive flavours are bright, layered, and persistent, and the acidity is clean, fresh, and zesty.

NOTES

....
....
....
....

NEW!

★ ★ ★ ★ ½

Columbia Crest 'Grand Estates' Chardonnay 2013

COLUMBIA VALLEY $17.95 (462846) 13.5% ALC.   XD

This really lovely chardonnay had a lot of love in the winery. It was 100 percent barrel-fermented, spent nine months on lees (dead yeast cells, which give complexity to the texture and flavours of wine) and was aged in new barrels (which are not cheap). The result is impressive, with loads of interesting flavours and texture, not to mention good balance and structure, and real style. Enjoy it with poultry, pork, white fish, and seafood.

NOTES

....
....
....

ARGENTINA

ARGENTINA IS THE WORLD'S fifth-largest wine producer, but it began to make its mark on the world wine scene only fifteen years ago. Although we see more and more quality and good-value wines from there, we haven't seen half of what Argentina can do. Wine producers (most located in the sprawling Mendoza region) make superlative reds and whites, and it's the reds that have grabbed more attention. Malbec, a red grape native to southwest France, has become Argentina's signature variety. Made in big and robust styles, the wine is a natural for beef, which just happens to be another of Argentina's major products. But cabernet sauvignons and other reds can be just as impressive.

Alamos Cabernet Sauvignon 2013
★ ★ ★ ★

MENDOZA $15.20 (295105) 13.5% ALC. **D**

Made from grapes growing in the foothills of the Andes, this shows the ripeness that cabernet sauvignon achieves in the sunny warmth. The flavours are robust, intense and well layered, and a seam of good, clean acidity gives the wine tanginess. This is definitely for hearty red meats like grilled steak and lamb.

NOTES
....
....
....
....

NEW!
★ ★ ★ ★
Alamos Malbec 2014

MENDOZA $15.20 (295139) 13.5% ALC. **XD**

Argentina made its name in the wine world with malbec, and there's a veritable ocean of it on the market. The trick lies is finding the quality examples that offer good value. This one delivers on the plush, plentiful fruit that is malbec's hallmark, and enhances it with good balance and structure. Supple tannins complete the picture, unless you want to add grilled meats as they so often do in Argentina: beef, of course, but also lamb and pork.

NOTES
....
....
....
....

★ ★ ★ ★
Argento Reserva Cabernet Sauvignon 2014

MENDOZA $13.95 (164764) 13.9% ALC. **XD**

Some of the most impressive wines I've tasted in Argentina were cabernet sauvignons. It's a variety that's been overshadowed by malbec. This one delivers plenty of rich fruit flavours that are deep and intense. They're nicely balanced by acidity, though, and the tannins are drying and manageable. Drink it with hearty red-meat dishes, game, and bison burgers.

NOTES
....
....
....
....

Catena Malbec 2014

★ ★ ★ ★ ★

MENDOZA $19.95 (478727) 13.5% ALC.   **D**

[Vintages Essential] Malbec from Argentina hit the wine world a bit like Australian shiraz did in the 1990s, and they often share a popular style: intense fruit flavours, generous texture, and easy-going acidity. This 100 percent malbec from Catena is a cut above many others. It delivers structure and balance along with power and intensity. The acidity is clean and refreshing, and lightens the weight of the fruit. It's a great wine for full-flavoured grilled red meats.

NOTES
....
....
....
....

Catena Cabernet Sauvignon 2014

★ ★ ★ ★ ★

MENDOZA $19.95 (985002) 13.9% ALC.   **XD**

[Vintages Essential] The label points out that the vines were grown at high altitudes—in this case about 1,000 to 1,500 metres above sea level. That means sunny days and cool temperatures, so that the grapes ripen well and develop good acidity. Taste them in the wine, where the flavours are ripe and concentrated and the acidity fresh and clean. The tannins are supple and fine, and this is an excellent choice for roasted and (especially) grilled red meats.

NOTES
....
....
....

Doña Paula Malbec 2014

★ ★ ★ ★ ★

UCO VALLEY, MENDOZA $16.15 (394783) 14.3% ALC.   **D**

The grapes for this wine were grown in the winery's Alluvia vineyard, at an altitude of 1350 metres above sea-level. It's a stylish malbec that's perfect for grilled red meats. You'll find it has finely nuanced flavours that are both broad in scope and deep in complexity, while clean and refreshing acidity plays counterpoint to the concentration of the fruit. The tannins are ripe and supple, and the components are well integrated.

NOTES
....
....
....

FuZion 'Alta' Reserva Cabernet Sauvignon 2014

★ ★ ★ ★

MENDOZA $10.05 (207357) 13.5% ALC.   **D**

Although known worldwide for malbec, Argentina produces exceptional cabernet sauvignon. This is a very well-priced, entry-level example, but it delivers well across the board. It's lively and fresh, carries ripe and sweet fruit with some complexity, and has modest tannins. It's a very good choice for burgers, ribs, and all kinds of grilled or braised red meat.

NOTES
....
....
....
....

FuZion 'Orgánico' Malbec/Cabernet 2014

★ ★ ★ ★

MENDOZA $13.10 (127456) 13% ALC.   **XD**

There are so many wines in the FuZion range that it can be confusing. Look for this one, though, an organic wine that delivers good quality across the board. It's full of ripe fruit, as you'd expect, and it's layered, plush, and, importantly, supported by a seam of fresh acidity. The tannins are moderate, and this goes well with Argentina's main meat, grilled beef.

NOTES
....
....
....
....
....

Graffigna 'Centenario' Reserve Malbec 2014

NEW!
★ ★ ★ ★ ½

SAN JUAN $13.95 (230474) 14.5% ALC.   **D**

This malbec delivers a really juicy texture that sets it up for food, and it's the sort of versatile red that goes well not only with red meats but also with poultry and pork and many hearty mushroom or tomato-based vegetarian dishes. It's almost astringently dry, with fresh acidity supporting the concentrated fruit. The tannins are ripe and drying.

NOTES
....
....
....
....
....

NEW!
★ ★ ★ ★ ½

Graffigna 'Centenario' Reserve Shiraz 2013

SAN JUAN $13.95 (164731) 14.5% ALC.   D

Although Argentina hit the wine world with malbec, other red varieties are often equally impressive. Not a lot of shiraz grows there, but many of the wines are well worth looking at. This example in the now-classic New World, fruit-forward style, is well-managed with layered fruit that's balanced by fresh acidity. The tannins recede from the palate, and this is an easy choice for red meats, burgers, and ribs—an easy-going wine for easy-going food.

NOTES
....
....
....
....

★ ★ ★ ★

La Mascota Cabernet Sauvignon 2013

MENDOZA $13.95 (292110) 14% ALC.   XD

Argentina produces many fine cabernet sauvignons, which go as well with the country's beef-heavy diet as the better-known malbecs. This full-bodied cabernet is very rich, with plush and concentrated flavours and a generous and smooth texture. But the acidity rides in to relieve the intensity of the fruit, making the wine remarkably food friendly. The tannins have a fairly strong grip, but some well-seasoned red meats, cooked no more than medium, will take care of them.

NOTES
....
....
....

★ ★ ★ ★ ★

Luigi Bosca Malbec 2013

MENDOZA $17.95 (79293) 14% ALC.   XD

[Vintages Essential] This malbec punches above its weight and is several cuts above many others at this price (and higher). Look for concentrated fruit with weight, structure, and attractive layering, and a good seam of acidity that lightens its impact. The tannins are ripe and drying. Everything holds together well, and this is a great choice for grilled red meats. It will age, too; you can safely hang on to it through 2020.

NOTES
....
....
....

NEW!
★★★★

Norton 'Barrel Select' Malbec 2014

MENDOZA $13.10 (400556) 14% ALC. **D**

This delivers all you expect of a mid-range Malbec—and a bit more.
The flavours are ripe-sweet at the core and well layered, with plenty
of complexity. For all that it's forward and concentrated, the fruit is
complemented by well-pitched acidity, making this versatile at the table.
Drink it with grilled red meats, as they do in Argentina, or with well-
seasoned sausages, burgers, or barbecued ribs.

NOTES

....

....

....

....

★★★★ ½

Pascual Toso 'Limited Edition' Malbec 2013

MENDOZA $16.20 (162610) 14% ALC. **XD**

This is a step or two above many malbecs at this price. It has all the rich
flavour that you expect of Argentine malbec, but the integration and
harmony of the components are notable. The fruit is ripe and focused, the
acidity well calibrated and the tannins supple. Dry and medium bodied,
it's a great choice for anything from a gourmet burger to a seasoned rack
of lamb.

NOTES

....

....

....

....

★★★★

Santa Julia Reserva Cabernet Sauvignon 2014

VALLED DE UCO, MENDOZA $13.05 (242370) 13.5% ALC. **D**

This is a well-made, straightforward cabernet that goes well with grilled
or roasted game and red meats—especially beef, the most popular meat in
Argentina. You'll find nicely concentrated flavours here, and they're well
balanced by the food-friendly acidity. The tannins are drying, ever-so-
slightly grippy, but easily managed.

NOTES

....

....

....

....

....

ARGENTINA | RED WINES

NEW!
★ ★ ★ ★ ½

Trapiche 'Broquel' Malbec 2014

MENDOZA $14.95 (234385) 14.5% ALC.   XD

Trapiche makes a lot of quality wines, among them this very attractive malbec that delivers the expected richness of fruit and enhances it with good structure and layered complexity. It approaches full bodied in weight, but it's lightened and freshened by clean acidity. The tannins are drying and relaxed. It's a natural for red meats but try it with full-flavoured cheeses, too.

NOTES
....
....
....
....
....

★ ★ ★ ★

Trapiche Reserve Malbec 2014

MENDOZA $12.10 (614651) 14% ALC.   XD

This is an attractive malbec that shows well-focused and -defined fruit from start to finish. The fruit is complex and quite structured, and the fruit-acid balance is well done, with the acidity coming through well to set the wine up for food. The tannins are easy-going, and this very drinkable malbec makes a great partner for red meats, burgers, and pizzas.

NOTES
....
....
....
....
....

AUSTRALIA

AUSTRALIA IS A REAL POWERHOUSE for red wine, and Australian shiraz dominated New World red wine exports for years. But although shiraz is regarded as Australia's king, other red varieties are very important, especially cabernet sauvignon, merlot, and pinot noir.

The most common geographical designation for Australian wine is South Eastern Australia. This isn't a state but a mega-zone that includes more than 90 percent of the country's wine production and most of its wine regions. Other appellations include states (such as Victoria and South Australia) and the many smaller regions. Among them, the best-known include Barossa Valley and McLaren Vale, both of which are represented in this list.

★ ★ ★ ★

19 Crimes Shiraz/Durif 2014

VICTORIA $19.15 (369777) 14.5% ALC.   D

It'd be a crime not to try this interesting blend. Durif is little-known but makes very interesting wines and here, blended with shiraz, it makes for an almost full-bodied blend with good structure and complexity. The balance is good and the tannins are moderate and manageable. This is a natural for a barbie, as these convicts' descendants call a barbecue. Grilled sausages, burgers, and ribs come to mind.

NOTES
....
....
....
....

★ ★ ★ ★ ★

Angus the Bull Cabernet Sauvignon 2013

CENTRAL VICTORIA $20.15 (602615) 14% ALC.   XD

Now and again a wine stands out from the herd, and Angus is one of them. It delivers generous, concentrated flavours that are complex and ripe, but well on this side of the fence that separates ripe from jammy. Full bodied and juicy with relaxed tannins, it's a great partner for . . . beef, of course. But don't be cowed by this, and don't let me steer you away from serving Angus with other red meats.

NOTES
....
....
....
....

NEW!
★ ★ ★ ★ ½

Fowles 'Farm to Table' Cabernet Merlot 2012

VICTORIA $14.95 (436964) 13.5% ALC.   XD

The "farm to table" (cutting out the retailer) movement is well established, as is "vineyard to table"—buying wine at the cellar door. You have to buy this from the LCBO and you'll find it worthwhile. Look for lovely flavours that are ripe and complex and in harmony with well-calibrated acid. The tannins are moderate and this is a natural for red meats, as the label (showing cuts of beef) implies.

NOTES
....
....
....
....

NEW!
★ ★ ★ ★ ½

Jacob's Creek 'Double Barrel' Shiraz Second Vintage

AUSTRALIA $19.95 (419986) 14.8% ALC.   D

The "Double Barrel" is not a shotgun but refers to the aging in two lots of barrels: first in conventional oak barrels, then in barrels previously used to age Scotch whisky. The latter raise the intensity and complexity of the fruit, as you'll see when you taste the wine. Beyond that, it's well structured and has very good balance and supple tannins. Drink it with well-seasoned red meats.

NOTES
....
....
....
....
....

NEW!
★ ★ ★ ★ ★

Jacob's Creek Reserve Cabernet Sauvignon 2013

COONAWARRA $16.95 (91751) 13.8% ALC.   XD

Coonawarra is Australia's best-known region for cabernet sauvignon, so it's not surprising to find that this wine attains such quality. There's loads of complexity in the flavours and they unfold as you sip. They're well-defined and structured, and supported by well-measured acidity. This is a very dry wine with grippy tannins, and it's an excellent partner for grilled red meats and game.

NOTES
....
....
....
....

NEW!
★ ★ ★ ★

Mallee Rock Shiraz/Cabernet Sauvignon 2014

LIMESTONE COAST $14.95 (434589) 14.5% ALC.   D

Limestone is often a magic word in the wine world as it underlies many prestigious regions. It's no guarantee of a quality wine, but here it has produced a red blend that shows concentrated, assertive fruit and well-balanced acidity. It's fairly astringent, there's decent complexity and structure, and it's an excellent choice for red meats generally, as well as for burgers and hearty dishes calling for red wine.

NOTES
....
....

....

Nugan Estate 'Alfredo' Second Pass Shiraz 2014

★ ★ ★ ★

AUSTRALIA $16.20 (368811) 14% ALC. D

The "second pass" in the name refers to the grape juice for this wine being
fermented on the skins left over from making Nugan's top-tier shiraz. This
adds to the rich, intense flavours you find here. They run right through
the palate, with deep complexity, and are balanced by clean acidity. The
tannins are drying and a bit grippy. Drink this with intensely flavoured
and weighty red meat and game.

NOTES
....
....
....
....

Penfolds 'Koonunga Hill' Shiraz/Cabernet 2013

★ ★ ★ ★ ½

SOUTH AUSTRALIA $18.20 (285544) 14% ALC. D

Although the shiraz/cabernet sauvignon blend is also made elsewhere,
Australia has made it its own, and this example shows the character
well. Look for rich, ripe fruit that's sweet at the core and has layers of
complexity with a tangy, fresh texture from the well-calibrated acidity. It's
dry with moderate tannins and it's a great partner for grilled red meats.

NOTES
....
....
....
....
....

Penfolds 'Thomas Hyland' Shiraz 2013

★ ★ ★ ★ ★

ADELAIDE $18.75 (611210) 14.5% ALC. D

[Vintages Essential] This big, luscious shiraz is named for the son-in-law
of Dr. Penfold, who founded the company. Thomas would be delighted
to be associated with it. It's an assertive red with intense fruit flavours and
has a texture that's plush, dense, and tangy. Between medium and full
bodied, it's a sheer pleasure to drink—especially with well-seasoned red
meat, like lamb with garlic and rosemary.

NOTES
....
....
....
....

Pirramimma Petit Verdot 2012

★ ★ ★ ★ ★

MCLAREN VALE $20.75 (986752) 13.5% ALC.   D

[Vintages Essential] Petit verdot is a variety often used in small percentages in Bordeaux reds, but here you get the real McCoy—a straight varietal wine that offers rich, well-structured flavours that are impressively complex and supported by good acidity. The tannins are firm and well integrated. This wine—which was one of my favourites for many years when it used to appear in Vintages—is made for well-seasoned red meats and game.

NOTES
....
....
....
....

Pirramimma 'Stock's Hill' GSM 2013

★ ★ ★ ★ ★

MCLAREN VALE $17.45 (352252) 14.7% ALC.   D

GSM stands for a blend of grenache, syrah/shiraz, and mourvèdre/mataro. (The initials work in Australia and Europe.) It originated in the Rhône Valley, but has been emulated in other regions. This iteration of the blend is richly and intensely flavoured, with impressive complexity and length. It's finely balanced, with a generous texture and supple tannins. It has some power and heft, and it's very well suited to red meats.

NOTES
....
....
....
....

Red Knot Cabernet Sauvignon 2014

★ ★ ★ ★ ½

MCLAREN VALE $18.15 (91702) 14% ALC.   XD

It's not so much a knot on the label as an impossibly tangled piece of . . . string? The wine itself is a lot easier to unravel. First you get very pleasant and complex aromas (if you bother to sniff it), then a mouthful of lovely, rich fruit that's concentrated, focused, and layered. The tannins are supple, the balance is right-on. What's not to like? And it's even better with red meat or a hearty mushroom risotto.

NOTES
....
....

Ringbolt Cabernet Sauvignon 2014

★ ★ ★ ★ ½

MARGARET RIVER $21.95 (606624) 14% ALC.   D

[Vintages Essential] Margaret River is one of the wine regions of Western Australia, an area that has developed a reputation for high-quality wines. This cabernet is one of them. You'll find it has concentrated and full-on flavours, but that they're focused, complex, and nicely balanced by the refreshing acidity. The tannins are ripe and supple. This is a great choice for grilled, roasted, or braised red meats.

NOTES

....

....

....

....

Rosemount Estate 'Diamond Label' Shiraz 2015

★ ★ ★ ★ ½

SOUTH AUSTRALIA $15.10 (302349) 13.5% ALC.   D

This is almost a classic Australian shiraz. It's been in the LCBO for many years, and the style has evolved perceptibly over time. It's all there: the rich, ripe flavours and the tangy texture that you expect. But it's not aggressive, not in your face. Instead, it's medium bodied with a dry, lightly tangy texture, has good structure, and is excellent with grilled lamb chops or roasted lamb.

NOTES

....

....

....

....

Stone Dwellers Cabernet Sauvignon 2013

★ ★ ★ ★ ★

STRATHBOGIE RANGES $20.20 (212761) 14% ALC.   XD

Made by the Fowles family (you'll find other wines by them in this book), this cabernet is full bodied but stylish and elegant. The fruit is ripe and forward, but it's nuanced and finely layered, and supported by lovely acidity that gives juiciness to the texture. The tannins are supple and ripe. This is a terrific pairing with grilled red meats such as a roast or rack of lamb studded with garlic and sprigs of rosemary.

NOTES

....

....

....

....

Wakefield 'Promised Land' Cabernet Sauvignon 2014

★ ★ ★ ★

SOUTH AUSTRALIA $14.95 (358838) 13.5% ALC. XD

Look for plenty of ripe, concentrated, and quite structured fruit here. It's well supported by a broad seam of fresh acidity, giving the wine some juiciness. The tannins are drying and slightly gripping, but quite manageable. This is a good choice for red meats in general, but it's not so weighty that you couldn't pair it with lighter dishes, such as herbed grilled pork chops or coq au vin.

NOTES

Wakefield 'Promised Land' Shiraz 2014

NEW!
★ ★ ★ ★

SOUTH AUSTRALIA $14.95 (441543) 13.5% ALC. XD

There are so many Australian shirazes it can be perplexing to sort out the good from the better. This is definitely in the "better" camp. You'll find it delivers the fruit-forwardness that's expected, but it also shows superior structure and balance, the marks of a better wine. You can pair this with casual meals such as burgers and ribs, or with steaks and rich winter stews (with or without meat).

NOTES

Wolf Blass Yellow Label Cabernet Sauvignon 2014

★ ★ ★ ★ ½

LANGHORNE CREEK/ $17.15 (251876) 13.5% ALC. XD
MCLAREN VALE

This is a really well-made and -balanced cabernet, and it's an excellent choice for grilled red meats, hearty stews, and casual meals of burgers or grilled seasoned sausages. The fruit is ripe and well defined, with a complex flavour profile that persists right through the palate. The acidity shines through clearly, giving the wine freshness, and the tannins are supple and easy-going.

NOTES

NEW!
★ ★ ★ ★ ½

Wolf Blass 'Gold Label' Syrah 2013

ADELAIDE HILLS $25.20 (399477) 14.5% ALC. **XD**

For some time Australian winemakers have been moving away from
the intense, jammy shirazes that were more popular in the 1990, and
embracing more balanced, food-friendlier styles. Labelling the wine
"syrah" signals a different style, and this one is concentrated, structured,
focused, and well balanced—it even reaches for elegance. This is a very
good choice for red meats and many hearty pasta dishes.

NOTES
....
....
....
....

NEW!
★ ★ ★ ★ ½

Yalumba 'Coonawarra' Cabernet Sauvignon 2015

COONAWARRA $19.95 (460a667) 14.9% ALC. **XD**

Coonawarra, in South Australia, is known as the source of many of
Australia's finest cabernet sauvignons, and you can add this one to the
list. It's full of ripe fruit in the best New World style, and you can add to
its qualities complexity, structure, and balance. Although it's young for a
quality cabernet, it's nicely integrated. This is a natural for red meats and
food of that ilk, if not that elk.

NOTES
....
....
....
....

BRITISH COLUMBIA

BRITISH COLUMBIA'S WINERIES—most of them located in the Okanagan Valley—produce a lot of high-quality and well-priced red wine. Unfortunately, hardly any of it makes its way to Ontario.

The VQA (Vintners Quality Alliance) classification on British Columbia wine labels means that the grapes were grown in the region specified and that the wine has been tested and tasted by a panel.

Mission Hill Reserve Cabernet Sauvignon 2013

★ ★ ★ ★ ★

VQA OKANAGAN VALLEY $29.95 (553321) 13% ALC. **XD**

[Vintages Essential] Mission Hill helped put the Okanagan Valley wine region on the map, and the company's attention to detail has kept it in the forefront of British Columbia wine production. This cabernet sauvignon is stylish and opulent. You'll find elegant fruit flavours that are finely nuanced and focused right through the palate, and refreshing acidity that contributes a rich, tangy texture. The tannins are drying and manageable. This wine is a bit more than medium bodied, and it goes beautifully with roasted or grilled red meats.

NOTES

....

....

....

....

BULGARIA

BULGARIA IS AN IMPORTANT wine-producing country that turns out some stunning reds, especially cabernet sauvignon and merlot. Unfortunately, few of them make their way to Canada, but there are some solid entry-level wines that represent good value.

Boyar 'Selection' Cabernet Sauvignon 2014

★ ★ ★ ★

REGIONAL WINE $8.95 (340851) 13% ALC D
THRACIAN VALLEY

This is a very solid, medium-bodied cabernet that goes well with roasted red meats, poultry, pork, and many pasta dishes and pizzas. The fruit is ripe and concentrated without being extracted, the flavours are attractive, fresh, and vibrant, and the acidity is clean and refreshing. It's very dry (I'd have classed it XD, rather than the LCBO's D), with drying and manageable tannins.

NOTES
....
....
....
....

CALIFORNIA

CALIFORNIA'S WINE INDUSTRY BEGAN in earnest in the 1850s soon after the Gold Rush subsided. The industry fell on hard times during Prohibition in the 1920s and early 1930s, but was given a boost when, in 1976, some California wines beat some of the most prestigious French wines in a blind tasting in Paris. California accounts for 90 percent of the wine produced in the United States and is fourth in world wine production, after France, Italy, and Spain.

California's varied growing conditions are suitable for many different grape varieties and wine styles. The state's signature grape is zinfandel (the excuse for many zin-fully bad puns), but cabernet sauvignon is more important in terms of production and sales. Other significant varieties are merlot and pinot noir.

Most of the value wines in this book are labelled "California," which means that producers can use grapes grown anywhere in the state. Important designated regions within the state include Napa Valley, Sonoma County, and Paso Robles.

Beringer 'Founder's Estate' Cabernet Sauvignon 2014

★ ★ ★ ★ ½

CALIFORNIA $18.25 (534263) 13.9% ALC.   XD

Beringer is the Napa Valley's oldest continuous wine producer, dating back to 1876. It stayed in business even during the dry days of Prohibition by making sacramental wine. This cabernet is delicious rather than spiritual, delivering a medium body, an intense and juicy texture, and solid fruit flavours with very good complexity. It's dry, the tannins are moderate and manageable, and it goes very well with steak and other red meats.

NOTES

Beringer 'Founder's Estate' Zinfandel 2013

★ ★ ★ ★

CALIFORNIA $17.95 (308205) 14.5% ALC.   D

There's plenty of concentrated fruit in this zinfandel, as you would expect, but it's not as overbearing as many zins. You'll find it well pitched, with a good level of complexity, and in very good balance with the acidity. It's dry, with slightly grippy tannins, but easy to drink. This is a very good choice for red meats, winter stews, gourmet burgers, and hearty tomato-based pasta dishes.

NOTES

Beringer 'Knights Valley' Cabernet Sauvignon 2013

★ ★ ★ ★ ★

KNIGHTS VALLEY $39.95 (352583) 13% ALC.   XD

[Vintages Essential] This is a stunning wine, vintage after vintage. It achieves the feat that distinguishes many fine wines of being both bold and stylish at the same time. The flavours are deep, broad, and intricately layered, the texture is plump, plush, and generous, and the acidity is beautifully handled. The tannins are still gripping, so you might decant it for two or three hours to enjoy with beef grilled or roasted no more than medium rare.

NOTES

NEW!
★ ★ ★ ★

Big House Red 2013

CALIFORNIA $13.15 (178632) 13.5% ALC   D

They're a little cagey about what's in this blend, but it works. This
is a popular red that delivers a lot for the price. The fruit is big and
concentrated, with plenty of flavour that's matched by the generous and
quite smooth texture. The acid balance is good, reining in the intensity of
the fruit, and the tannins are relaxed. Enjoy this with red meats, burgers,
barbecued ribs, and (in the awful season) hearty stews.

NOTES
....
....
....
....

NEW!
★ ★ ★ ★

Big House 'Cardinal Zin' Zinfandel 2013

CALIFORNIA $13.10 (272401) 13.5% ALC.   D

This is a very zinny zinfandel, with the classic flavour profile centred on
dense, ripe fruit. What isn't zinny is the alcohol, which is low for varietal
zinfandels that routinely push well above 14 percent. What you get here is
fruit forwardness that's positive rather than assertive, a good acid balance,
and decent structure. It's a very good choice for grilled red meats, burgers,
grilled sausages, and barbecued ribs.

NOTES
....
....
....
....

NEW!
★ ★ ★ ★ ★

Bonterra Cabernet Sauvignon 2014

MENDOCINO, LAKE, AND $19.95 (342428) 12.1% ALC.   XD
SAN LUIS OBISPO COUNTIES

Some wines are blends of varieties, others are blends of barrels, and
yet others (like this one) are blends of different regions, each of which
produces a different style of cabernet. The blend works extremely well
here, producing impressive complexity in the well-defined fruit, exemplary
fruit-acid balance, and supple tannins. This is a great choice for red meats
of many kinds.

NOTES
....
....
....

NEW!
★★★★ ½   **Buried Hope Cabernet Sauvignon 2012**

NORTH COAST $19.95 (356113) 14.5% ALC.   D

It's no great surprise to find a full-bodied, fruit-assertive cabernet from California, but this one stands out from many because it shows very good complexity, structure, and balance—it's not just fruit, fruit, and more fruit. Look for very good layering and well-measured acid that reins in the fruit intensity. That said, it's a big wine that needs big food in the form of well-seasoned red and game meats.

NOTES
....
....
....
....

★★★★★   **Chateau St. Jean Pinot Noir 2013**

CALIFORNIA $20.20 (308221) 13.8% ALC.   D

This is a lovely pinot noir, definitely in a West Coast style, with solid fruit that's well focused, nicely complex, and structured. The acidity shines through and gives the wine some fresh juiciness, and the tannins are ripe and present yet understated. It's an excellent choice for charcuterie, roast turkey and chicken, roast and grilled pork, and grilled seasoned sausages.

NOTES
....
....
....
....

★★★★ ½   **Cline Zinfandel 2013**

LODI $16.45 (489278) 14% ALC.   D

This is a very good example of a zinfandel made to go with food. Unlike too many high-octane, high-performance zins that leave food in the dust, this one has a refreshing texture (not a heavy, low-acid one), and the concentrated ripe flavours are layered. It's medium bodied and the very dry texture works well with its fruitiness. The alcohol is well integrated and imperceptible on the nose and palate. This is a natural for well-seasoned red meats.

NOTES
....
....
....
....

Clos du Bois Cabernet Sauvignon 2013

★ ★ ★ ★ ½

NORTH COAST $16.95 (308304) 13.5% ALC. **D**

This is a big-bodied, fruit-forward cabernet that's dry and full of ripe fruit flavour from attack to long finish. It's well balanced, with a broad seam of clean acidity holding the weight of the fruit in check, and contributing tanginess to the texture. The tannins are easy-going. This is a natural for grilled steaks and other red meats and, at the barbecue, for burgers and well-seasoned sausages.

NOTES

....

....

....

....

Dreaming Tree 'Crush' Red 2013

★ ★ ★ ★

CALIFORNIA $18.15 (310391) 13.5% ALC. **D**

Mostly merlot and zinfandel, this is an easy-drinking red blend that offers plenty of ripe fruit flavours and good fruit-acid balance. It's dry, but there's a little sweetness in the flavours, and as an added bonus, you get decent complexity and good structure. This is a red wine you can drink on its own, but you can also easily pair it with well-seasoned red meats, burgers, and spicy sausages.

NOTES

....

....

....

....

NEW!
★ ★ ★ ★

Enigma Cabernet Sauvignon 2014

CALIFORNIA $13.95 (428847) 13.5% ALC. **D**

This is a dry cabernet made in an easy-drinking style. It doesn't rely on sweetness to achieve that, as many reds now do, but on a lower level of acidity with a texture that's mouth filling, round, and above all, soft. This one almost caresses your palate, but it still offers some complexity and structure, and the tannins are drying but easy-going. Drink it with burgers, barbecued ribs, and grilled sausages.

NOTES

....

....

....

....

NEW!
★ ★ ★ ★ ½

Fetzer 'Eagle Peak' Merlot 2013

CALIFORNIA $13.90 (341131) 13.5% ALC. D

A fairly robust merlot, this delivers assertive, up-front fruit and speaks
what many people think California wine is all about. But it's no fruit
bomb. It's well structured, with good complexity and layering, and the
acidity reins in the fruit intensity well. The tannins are supple and relaxed.
Drink it with red meats, as well as with burgers, grilled sausages, and
barbecued ribs.

NOTES
....
....
....
....

★ ★ ★ ★

Gnarly Head Cabernet Sauvignon 2013

CALIFORNIA $14.95 (68924) 14.5% ALC. D

The label shows a stylized and very gnarly grapevine, making you think
this could be from old vines. There's no such claim, but the wine has the
concentrated flavour you often expect from more-mature vines. Look
for intense, sweet fruit flavours here, with a generous texture and drying
tannins. It's medium to full in weight and goes with heavier dishes like
steak.

NOTES
....
....
....
....

NEW!
★ ★ ★ ★ ½

Hahn GSM 2014

CENTRAL COAST $18.95 (441568) 14.5% ALC. D

GSM is short for a common blend of grenache, syrah, and mourvèdre,
originally found in the southern Rhône Valley in France. It's been
emulated in many other places, and this example from California shows
its versatility. The flavours are very concentrated, with impressive layering,
and they're lightened by fresh acidity. The tannins are drying but easy-
going, and this is a very good choice for many red-meat dishes.

NOTES
....
....
....
....

Hahn Pinot Noir 2014

★ ★ ★ ★ ½

MONTEREY COUNTY $19.20 (226555) 14.5% ALC.   D

This is distinctly in the style known as "New World," with the fruit upfront—fruit that's positive, complex, and persistent right through the palate. It's paired with the fresh acidity that's the hallmark of successful pinot noir, and shows easy-going tannins. Ready to drink on its own, this goes well with roast lamb, pork, and poultry, as well as with grilled salmon and hearty vegetarian dishes like mushroom risotto.

NOTES

J. Lohr 'Seven Oaks' Cabernet Sauvignon 2013

★ ★ ★ ★ ½

PASO ROBLES $22.95 (656561) 13.5% ALC.   D

[Vintages Essential] Named for a vineyard that has seven oak trees growing in it, this well-balanced cabernet sauvignon shows lovely, ripe fruit flavours that are well defined and layered. A broad seam of fresh acidity contributes an attractive tangy texture, and the tannins are easy-going. This is a great choice for grilled or roasted red meats, as well as for many full-flavoured vegetarian dishes, such as mushroom risotto.

NOTES

NEW!
★ ★ ★ ★

Kenwood Sonoma County Zinfandel 2013

SONOMA COUNTY $19.95 (350462) 14.5% ALC.   D

This is a robust red, as you expect a zinfandel to be, but it's not as hefty and big bodied as many zinfandels are. Look for good structure and fruit-acid balance, with some freshness in the texture. The fruit itself is concentrated and has some depth, but it delivers complexity too. The alcohol is mid-range for zinfandel, and not at all perceptible. Overall, it's a successful wine and a good partner for red meats, burgers, and hearty winter stews.

NOTES

Liberty School Cabernet Sauvignon 2013

★★★★★

PASO ROBLES $21.95 (738823) 13.5% ALC.   **D**

[Vintages Essential] This 100 percent cabernet is one of the great buys in the LCBO at this price point; it over-delivers on everything and clearly states its California pedigree. Look for concentrated, forward, and ripe flavours with plenty of structure and complexity; a generous, mouth-filling, tangy texture; soft, sweet tannins; and a finish that stays with you. It's a natural for rich red-meat dishes.

NOTES

....

....

....

....

Liberty School Zinfandel 2010

★★★★★

PASO ROBLES $19.95 (41095) 13.5% ALC.   **D**

[Vintages Essential] This is a delicious zinfandel that shows all the intensity and depth of fruit you expect from the variety. The fruit is ripe and sweet, but it's reined in by a good dose of acidity that lightens the texture of the wine. With nice layering and good structure, this wine goes well with well-seasoned grilled red meats, gourmet burgers, and spicy barbecued sausages.

NOTES

....

....

....

....

Louis M. Martini Cabernet Sauvignon 2013

★★★★★

NAPA VALLEY $32.95 (232371) 14.2% ALC.   **D**

[Vintages Essential] This is almost a classic example of the modern Napa style of cabernet. It delivers the power that "Napa cab" implies (never a Ford Focus cab, but a Mercedes), but along with the heft and depth you get breadth and structure. The alcohol is as integrated as the fresh acidity and slightly grippy tannins. This is a natural for a grilled well-seasoned steak or a rack of lamb prepared with garlic and rosemary.

NOTES

....

....

....

....

Louis M. Martini Cabernet Sauvignon 2014

★ ★ ★ ★

SONOMA COUNTY $19.15 (292151) 14% ALC.   **XD**

The name "Martini" might not seem that promising for a winery—
can you imagine James Bond asking for "a Martini cab, shaken not
stirred"?—but the results are what's important. This is a lovely cabernet,
with concentrated and well-defined flavours that are consistent from start
to long finish. It's well balanced, with supple, easily approached tannins,
and it goes well with all manner of red meats and other hearty dishes.

NOTES
....
....
....
....

McManis Cabernet Sauvignon 2014

★ ★ ★ ★ ½

CALIFORNIA $19.95 (212126) 13.5% ALC.   **XD**

[Vintages Essential] This is a full-bodied cabernet that delivers rich
flavours that are both broad in scope and deep in complexity. They're
reined in by clean, refreshing acidity that adds some juiciness to the
texture, and they're framed by supple, ripe tannins. It's a delicious red that
goes really well with grilled steak and lamb, but it suits grilled red meats
and game across the board.

NOTES
....
....
....
....

Meiomi Pinot Noir 2014

★ ★ ★ ★ ½

MONTEREY/SONOMA/ $26.95 (130138) 14.5% ALC.   **D**
SANTA BARBARA COUNTIES

This wine is a blend of regions, rather than varieties, where each region
contributes pinot with a different character to the whole. Look for ripe,
plush fruit with a multi-dimensional flavour profile that reflects the
different sources. The acidity is clean and fresh, the tannins have a relaxed
grip, and this is a fine choice for grilled lamb or duck, and for wild
mushroom risotto.

NOTES
....
....
....

Ménage à Trois 'Midnight' Dark Red Blend 2014

CALIFORNIA $18.45 (434597) 13.5% ALC.   D

It's definitely darker than most red wines, and it's packed with rich, fleshy fruit flavours. "Fruity" doesn't quite capture it. The texture is mouth filling and very round and smooth, and this character is accentuated by the quite low acidity—but not so low that it's not enjoyable. The tannins are relaxed. You can drink this on its own or with well-seasoned red meats.

NOTES

....

....

....

....

★★★★

Ménage à Trois Red 2014

CALIFORNIA $17.45 (308007) 13.5% ALC.   D

Made from zinfandel, merlot, and cabernet sauvignon, you'd expect this to be a big-boned wine, and it is. The flavours are broad and deep, with a core of real sweetness—a style with a big following—and they're solid right through. The tannins are easy-going and the acidity holds the weight of the fruit in check. The weight and intensity of this blend points it toward heavier, sweeter foods, so try it with burgers or barbecued ribs.

NOTES

....

....

....

....

★★★★

Mirassou Pinot Noir 2014

CALIFORNIA $14.45 (185249) 13.5% ALC.   D

This is a light-to-medium-bodied and easy-drinking pinot noir that goes well with poultry, pork, and grilled salmon, and also with many tomato-based pasta dishes. The flavours are fruity and bright, well-focused, and nicely concentrated. The acidity is clean and refreshing and the tannins are easy-going.

NOTES

....

....

....

....

Pepperwood Grove 'Old Vine' Zinfandel 2013

NEW!
★ ★ ★ ★

CALIFORNIA $13.95 (308163) 14% ALC. D

This is a lighter style of Zinfandel, but it still delivers the concentrated flavours you expect of the variety thanks in part to the old vines, which generally bear less but more intensely flavoured fruit. The acidity is well done, giving some freshness to the wine, and the tannins are relaxed. You can drink this with red meats, of course, but it's versatile enough to extend to pork and richer poultry dishes.

NOTES

Ravenswood 'Old Vine Vintners Blend' Zinfandel 2013

★ ★ ★ ★ ½

CALIFORNIA $18.95 (359257) 13.6% ALC. D

[Vintages Essential] If there's such a thing as a classic California zinfandel, this wine, with its plush, ripe fruit flavours, might be it. But it's also dry and moderately tannic, and it has an elegance you don't always find in the more common high-octane zinfandels. This one is full flavoured to be sure, but it's light on its feet and has a clean, fresh texture that makes it especially good for food. Open this, summer or winter, when you're serving grilled red meats.

NOTES

Robert Mondavi Cabernet Sauvignon 2013

★ ★ ★ ★ ★

NAPA VALLEY $35.95 (255513) 14.3% ALC. D

[Vintages Essential] How much should you pay for a Napa cab? Only the fare shown on the meter. The tariff here is a bit more than you usually find in the LCBO, but this is a delicious cabernet that's well worth the price. It's elegant and stylish right through, with luscious and complex flavours. It's dry and medium bodied, with moderate tannins and a sleek and quite refreshing texture. Serve it with rack of lamb or other grilled red meat.

NOTES

★ ★ ★ ★ **Robert Mondavi 'Private Selection'**
Cabernet Sauvignon 2014

CENTRAL COAST $17.95 (392225) 13.5% ALC. **XD**

The "Private Selection" series delivers quality and value, and this cabernet sauvignon fits into the range effortlessly. The flavours are concentrated and nicely layered, the texture is generous and smooth (but refreshing), and the tannins are firm and manageable. This is a natural for roasted or grilled red meats, but it extends to rich pasta dishes and aged cheddar and other sharp cheeses.

NOTES
....
....
....
....

★ ★ ★ ★ **Robert Mondavi 'Private Selection' Merlot 2014**

CENTRAL COAST $18.95 (524769) 13.5% ALC. **D**

This is a quite luscious merlot that shows a smooth, almost plush texture, but the well-managed acidity cuts through to contribute food-friendly tanginess that verges on juiciness. It moderates the intensity of the ripe and nicely layered fruit, and the whole is framed by tannins that are ripe, supple, and very approachable. This is a merlot suited to red meats, grilled or roasted, and to hearty stews of many kinds.

NOTES
....
....
....
....

★ ★ ★ ★ **Robert Mondavi 'Private Selection' Pinot Noir 2014**

CALIFORNIA $18.95 (465435) 13.5% ALC. **D**

This pinot noir is a real pleasure to drink, and it lives up to the quality that the Mondavi name is associated with. You'll find it has quite intense and vibrant flavours of fresh, ripe fruit, with a smooth, easy-drinking texture and light tannins. Dry and medium bodied, it's a fine choice for grilled planked salmon or for roast turkey or chicken with cranberries.

NOTES
....
....
....
....

Smoking Loon 'Old Vine' Zinfandel 2013

NEW!
★★★★

CALIFORNIA $14.95 (272393) 14% ALC.   **D**

Why is this loon smoking? Because this is a smokin' zin? It's certainly full
of the rich, sweet, and layered fruit flavours you expect of zinfandel, and
it's also well structured and balanced. The tannins are quite relaxed and
manageable. Drink this with grilled red meats at the cottage while you're
listening for the loons to call. Can't hear them? It's because they've taken
up smoking and can't call with cigars in their beaks.

NOTES

Stags' Leap Cabernet Sauvignon 2013

★★★★★

NAPA VALLEY $49.95 (996405) 13.9% ALC.   **XD**

[Vintages Essential] This very attractive cabernet verges on elegant and
it shows why the variety became so closely identified with the region that
"Napa cab" seems a natural pairing. You can also pair this with red meats
to take advantage of its good weight and texture and the ripe, moderately
grippy tannins. The flavours are concentrated and layered and show as
much depth as breadth, and they're harnessed to fresh, food-friendly
acidity.

NOTES

Sterling 'Vintner's Collection' Cabernet Sauvignon 2013

★★★★

CENTRAL COAST $16.00 (56366) 13.5% ALC.   **D**

This is a fine medium-to-full-bodied cabernet that delivers rich and quite
luscious fruit all through the palate. For all the weight in the fruit, it's
relatively easy drinking because of the well-calibrated acidity, and to that
we must add good structure and complexity. It's an easy choice for grilled
or roasted red meats (including burgers) and for hearty winter stews.

NOTES

Sterling Napa Valley Cabernet Sauvignon 2013

★ ★ ★ ★ ½

NAPA VALLEY $29.95 (314575) 12.5% ALC. D

[Vintages Essential] Another Napa cabernet, this one is characterized by intense flavours that are solid right through the palate and out the other side. Look for good layering and structure, medium-plus body, and a smooth texture with easy-going tannins. It's almost a textbook cabernet. Drink it with roasted or grilled red meats, savoury sausages, or gourmet beef- or game- burgers.

NOTES

....

....

....

....

Sterling Napa Valley Merlot 2013

★ ★ ★ ★ ½

NAPA VALLEY $16.75 (330241) 13.5% ALC. D

[Vintages Essential] Napa merlot is too often overshadowed by better-known cabernet sauvignon (the "Napa cab" thing), but the region turns out excellent merlots, too. This one is characterized by concentrated, generous, and well-defined fruit, with very good complexity and structure. The acidity clicks in, fresh and clean, and the tannins are ripe, supple, and drying. It's an excellent choice for grilled lamb and other red meats.

NOTES

....

....

....

....

Wente 'Southern Hills' Cabernet Sauvignon 2013

★ ★ ★ ★ ½

LIVERMORE VALLEY/ $18.95 (301507) 13.5% ALC. D
SAN FRANCISCO BAY

These regions near San Francisco were first planted with vines by Spanish missionaries in the 1760s. The Wente family arrived a little later, in the 1840s. Powerful, intense, and full of layers of rich fruit flavour, this full-bodied cabernet delivers a texture that's mouth-filling and refreshing. The tannins are firm but manageable. This is a great choice when you're eating red meat grilled or roasted no more than medium rare.

NOTES

....

....

....

Woodbridge Cabernet Sauvignon 2014

★ ★ ★ ★ ½

CALIFORNIA $13.45 (48611) 13.5% ALC. D

Woodbridge is a Robert Mondavi brand that's designed to give good quality at a good price—good value, in other words. And this cabernet achieves the goal by delivering solid fruit flavours and nice balance. It's medium bodied and dry, has a soft, low-tannin texture, and goes very well with burgers and grilled red meats.

NOTES

....

....

....

....

CHILE

CHILE PRODUCES MANY OF THE BEST-VALUE red wines in the LCBO. They tend to be full of flavour and are often well structured. Important varieties include carmenère (Chile's signature variety), cabernet sauvignon, merlot, shiraz/syrah, and pinot noir, as well as blends.

What makes Chile such a good source for quality red wine? Climate and location are the keys. Most Chilean wine regions are in warm, sun-soaked but well-ventilated valleys. And more and more vineyards are being planted at higher altitudes to capture cooler conditions that promote fresh acidity in the grapes. Maipo and Colchagua are two of these valleys, and they're both well represented among the wines here. As Chile's wines gain the following they deserve and sales increase, expect prices to do the same. In the meantime, enjoy Chile's reds for their great quality and value at lower prices.

Designated Chilean wine regions are indicated after the letters DO *(Denominación de Origen)*.

Caliterra Reserva Cabernet Sauvignon 2014

★ ★ ★ ★

DO COLCHAGUA VALLEY $10.05 (257329) 13.5% ALC.   **D**

This is a basic, uncomplicated cabernet sauvignon that presents solid fruit flavours with moderate complexity and good fruit-acid balance. It's quite dry, with negligible tannins, and has a tangy texture. It's a good choice for burgers and barbecued ribs, and generally for any red meat from the grill.

NOTES

....

....

....

....

....

Carmen Gran Reserva Cabernet Sauvignon 2012

★ ★ ★ ★ ★

DO MAIPO VALLEY $16.95 (358309) 14% ALC.   **XD**

The Maipo Valley is recognized as one of *the* best areas, if not the best area, in Chile for cabernet sauvignon. It's cooled by the Andean winds and the cabernets are as fresh as they can be powerful. This example shows impressive complexity, with concentrated and defined fruit and a sleek, fresh texture that's framed by supple tannins. It's a natural for well-seasoned red meats.

NOTES

....

....

....

....

....

Carmen 'Premier' Reserva Carmenère 2015

★ ★ ★ ★

DO COLCHAGUA VALLEY $11.95 (169052) 13.5% ALC.   **D**

In Chile, carmenère was long thought to be a variant of merlot until 1994, when it was identified in one of the vineyards of the Carmen winery that makes this wine. (There's no relationship between Carmen and carmenère.) This example is full of concentrated fruit and shows good balance and some complexity. It's plush and fruity and it goes well with red meats and grilled spicy sausages.

NOTES

....

....

....

....

NEW!
★ ★ ★ ★ ½

Concha y Toro 'Casillero del Diablo' Carmenère 2014

DO CENTRAL VALLEY $13.95 (620666) 13.5% ALC.   XD

The "666" in the product code can't be a coincidence for a wine in the
"Devil's Cellar" series. And what did the devil call when he wanted a
victim to enter his cellar? "Carmenère!" It all adds up to a diabolically
good wine for the price. You'll find expressive and forward fruit, good
balance, and relaxed tannins. It's a great option for sitting around a
barbecue with friends, doing nothing in particular. You know the saying:
"idle hands do the devil's work."

NOTES

NEW!
★ ★ ★ ★ ½

**Concha y Toro 'Casillero del
Diablo' Devil's Collection Reserva Red 2014**

CHILE $14.95 (436956) 13.5% ALC.   D

A blend of syrah (65 percent), cabernet sauvignon (20 percent), and
carmenère (15 percent), this is a robust, full-bodied red that's an excellent
choice for well-seasoned game and red-meat dishes. The fruit is up-front
and generous all the way through, and it's well balanced by the fresh
acidity needed to make it a successful partner with food. The structure is
good and the easy-going tannins stay well in the background.

NOTES

NEW!
★ ★ ★ ★ ★

**Concha y Toro 'Marques de
Casa Concha' Cabernet Sauvignon 2014**

DO MAIPO VALLEY $21.95 (337238) 13.5% ALC.   XD

[Vintages Essential] This is a stunning cabernet sauvignon that shows
why the Maipo Valley is thought to be the best location for the variety in
Chile. The fruit is optimally ripe, concentrated, and with a ripe-sweet core
that dominates the impressive layering. It's freshened by clean acidity, and
the tannins are supple and well integrated. This is a great choice for well-
seasoned red meats such as steaks and lamb chops.

NOTES

Concha y Toro 'Winemaker's Lot 148' Carmenère 2014

★ ★ ★ ★ ★

DO RAPEL VALLEY $17.95 (30957) 14% ALC. XD

[Vintages Essential] This is a full-bodied red that delivers all the depth of fruit that carmenère is known for. In addition to flavours that hold steady and firm right through the palate, look for good structure here, along with good fruit-acid balance and easy-going tannins. It's a lovely red to pair with many well-seasoned grilled or roasted red meats, as well as with barbecued ribs.

NOTES
....
....
....
....
....

Cono Sur 'Bicicleta' Pinot Noir 2013

★ ★ ★ ★ ½

CHILE $11.10 (341602) 14% ALC. D

Cono Sur is by far Chile's biggest producer of pinot noir. This one has the intense flavour you expect from a Chilean wine, but it's subtle enough to capture the classic textures and character of the variety. Look for concentrated flavours and a lively, food-friendly texture. Dry and medium bodied, it has light tannins and goes very well with grilled salmon or lamb.

NOTES
....
....
....

NEW!
★ ★ ★ ★ ½

Novas Gran Reserva Carmenère/Cabernet Sauvignon 2013

DO COLCHAGUA VALLEY $16.00 (434662) 14.5% ALC. XD

This blend is 85 percent carmenère and 15 percent cabernet sauvignon, sourced from organically farmed vineyards. Partially aged in oak barrels, it retains a lot of fruit purity, and the flavours are both bright and serious, with depth as much as breadth. The fruit-acid balance is very good, and the tannins are supple. It's a natural for hearty red-meat dishes.

NOTES
....
....
....
....
....

★ ★ ★ ★   **Errazuriz 'Estate Series' Cabernet Sauvignon 2014**

DO MAIPO & $14.10 (262717) 13.5% ALC.   **D**
ACONCAGUA VALLEYS

Errazuriz recently opened one of the most impressive wineries in Chile.
Some of the fruit for this wine comes from the surrounding vineyards,
but most comes from Maipo, Chile's best region for cabernet sauvignon.
You'll find plenty of ripe, layered, and nicely structured fruit in this
bottle. It's persistent from start to finish and it's supported by clean,
refreshing acidity. The tannins are easy-going. Pair it with grilled or
roasted red meats.

NOTES

....

....

....

....

★ ★ ★ ★   **Errazuriz 'Estate Series' Pinot Noir 2014**

DO ACONCAGUA VALLEY $13.95 (226696) 13.5% ALC.   **D**

This is an attractive pinot noir that's very versatile with food. Try it with
pork and poultry, with grilled Atlantic salmon, with many tomato-based
Italian dishes, or with coq au vin. The flavours are well focused and quite
concentrated, and they're lifted by clean, fresh acidity. The balance is good
and the tannins are drying and approachable.

NOTES

....

....

....

....

★ ★ ★ ★ ½   **Errazuriz 'Max Reserva' Cabernet Sauvignon 2014**

DO ACONCAGUA VALLEY $19.15 (335174) 14% ALC.   **XD**

This is a fruit-forward cabernet with concentrated, well-layered, and
persistent flavours from start to finish. It's well structured and the fruit-
acid balance is good, with the acidity complementing the weight of the
fruit effectively. The tannins are easy-going. Enjoy this cabernet with
barbecued red meats and well-seasoned sausages.

NOTES

....

....

....

....

Las Mulas Reserva Cabernet Sauvignon 2014

★★★★½

DO CENTRAL VALLEY $12.95 (407494) 13.5% ALC.   **D**

This is a plush-textured, full-fruited cabernet that goes well with many red-meat dishes, as well as barbecued ribs. The fruit is quite dense and rich, the acidity is well measured, and the tannins are drying and easily managed. Made by the reliable Torres company, this is a very attractive cabernet made in a popular style.

NOTES

....

....

....

....

Luis Felipe Edwards Reserva Shiraz/Cabernet Sauvignon 2014

★★★★½

DO COLCHAGUA VALLEY $12.95 (308189) 14% ALC.   **D**

Luis Felipe Edwards grows some of his vines at high elevations (900 metres above sea level), where they benefit from conditions that are cooler than the valley floor. Call these wines "wines with altitude." This blend delivers quite bold flavours, good complexity, and acidity that delivers some fresh juiciness. The tannins are moderate, and you can easily pair this with burgers and many red-meat dishes.

NOTES

....

....

....

....

Montes 'Alpha' Cabernet Sauvignon 2013

★★★★★

DO COLCHAGUA VALLEY $19.95 (322586) 14% ALC.   **XD**

[Vintages Essential] This is an impressive cabernet sauvignon from one of Chile's top wineries. It's full bodied, with fruit that displays depth of complexity and breadth flavour right through the palate. Look for very good structure, freshness in the texture, and supple, manageable tannins. It's very well integrated and harmonious, and it's a natural for grilled red meats and game.

NOTES

....

....

....

....

Montes Reserva Cabernet Sauvignon 2014
★ ★ ★ ★ ★

DO COLCHAGUA VALLEY $12.95 (157883) 13.5% ALC. XD

In one of the barrel rooms at the Montes winery, the barrels are serenaded by Gregorian chants, 24/7. Maybe you can pick up the echoes here. If not, you'll still be happy with the intense flavours, complexity and depth of the fruit, the moderately gripping tannins, and the excellent fruit-acid balance. This is a terrific choice for steak and other grilled red meats, as well as stronger cheeses.

NOTES

Montes 'Twins' Malbec/Cabernet Sauvignon 2013
★ ★ ★ ★ ½

DO COLCHAGUA VALLEY $12.95 (352054) 14% ALC. D

The twins are, of course, the two grape varieties, although they're anything but identical twins. The malbec gives fruit and smooth richness to the wine, while the cabernet contributes structure, depth, and some tannins. Together it's a great, balanced combination of flavour and texture, ready to drink now with grilled red meats and hearty meaty meals.

NOTES

MontGras Reserva Cabernet Sauvignon 2014
★ ★ ★ ★ ½

DO CENTRAL VALLEY $11.95 (619205) 13.5% ALC. D

This is an impressive cabernet, full of rich, plush, concentrated fruit that's layered and that shows good structure. It's full bodied and dry, with moderate tannins, and it has a texture that manages to be plump and mouth-filling yet fresh at the same time. Think of this when you're serving well-seasoned grilled or roasted red meats, but at this price you can pour it for weekday burgers.

NOTES

NEW!
★★★★

MontGras Reserva Carmenère 2014

DO CENTRAL VALLEY $11.95 (178624) 13.5% ALC.   XD

Full of up-front, positive, and pungent fruit flavours, this delivers good complexity and structure. Look for plenty of nuances on the palate, with fruit that stays consistent from start to finish. The acidity balances the fruit effectively, and the tannins are relaxed. This is a fruity red that goes well with burgers, grilled sausages, and barbecued ribs.

NOTES

....
....
....
....

★★★★★

Pérez Cruz Reserva Cabernet Sauvignon 2012

DO MAIPO ALTO VALLEY $14.95 (694208) 14.5% ALC.   XD

[Vintages Essential] Vintage after vintage, this opulent cabernet sauvignon from Chile's key cabernet region is full of delicious layered flavours. You can smell the rich aromas as you pour the wine into your glass. The texture is full, smooth, and generous. For all its complexity, this is a dry wine with moderate tannins. It's perfect with well-seasoned red meat, like lamb with garlic and rosemary.

NOTES

....
....
....
....

★★★★★

Santa Carolina 'Reserva de Familia' Cabernet Sauvignon 2013

DO MAIPO VALLEY $18.95 (408658) 14.5% ALC.   XD

[Vintages Essential] The Maipo Valley is the source of many of Chile's great cabernet sauvignons, so it's no surprise to see it here. This is a beautiful cabernet in a modern style. It delivers forward fruit that's defined and nuanced and well proportioned to the fresh, juicy acidity. The tannins are sleek and supple, and this makes a great partner for grilled and roasted red meats.

NOTES

....
....
....
....

Santa Digna Reserve Cabernet Sauvignon 2013

★ ★ ★ ★ ½

DO CENTRAL VALLEY $15.10 (323881) 14% ALC.   XD

From Chile's big Central Valley region, this 100 percent cabernet delivers rich, plush, and layered flavours, complemented and reined in by acidity that translates as a tangy texture. Dry, with moderate and supple tannins, it goes well with seasoned red meat, like a New York strip loin and a shake or two of steak spice. It's a certified fair trade wine.

NOTES
....
....
....
....
....

NEW!
★ ★ ★ ★ ½   **Santa Rita 'Medalla Real' Reserva Carmenère 2012**

DO COLCHAGUA VALLEY $17.85 (392720) 14% ALC.   XD

This is a plush, fruit-forward carmenère that delivers very well across the board. Look for plenty of complexity and good structure in the rich fruit, which is effectively balanced by fresh, clean acidity. The tannins are relaxed and easy-going. It's a very good partner for well-seasoned or spicy red meats, as well as for burgers and ribs.

NOTES
....
....
....
....

NEW!
★ ★ ★ ★   **Santa Rita Reserva Carmenère 2015**

DO RAPEL VALLEY $13.95 (177774) 13.5% ALC.   D

This is a solid carmenère that's a great choice for summer barbecues and for casual dining year-round. Think of it when you're serving grilled sausages, burgers, or barbecued ribs, although it partners well with red meats generally. The flavours are full and consistent, the acidity is clean and balanced, and the tannins are relaxed.

NOTES
....
....
....
....

FRANCE

FRANCE IS THE WORLD'S LARGEST and one of the most important wine producers, and has scores of wines in the LCBO. For many years, French wine was widely believed to be the best in the world, and wines from Bordeaux, Burgundy, and Champagne were held up as the only wines worth drinking if you wanted to taste excellence. That's no longer so, as wine lovers have discovered the great wines made elsewhere. However, France continues to make high-quality and value-priced wine, as this list shows.

French wine labels display a few terms worth knowing. Wines labelled *Appellation d'Origine Contrôlée* (abbreviated AOC in this book) or *Appellation d'Origine Protégée* (AOP) have the highest-quality classification in France. They're made under tight rules that regulate the grape varieties that can be used, maximum yield per hectare, minimum alcohol, and so on.

Wines labelled *Vin de Pays* or IGP *(Indication Géographique Protégée)* are regional wines made with fewer restrictions. They must be good quality, but producers have more flexibility in the grapes they can use and how much wine they can make per hectare of vineyard. *Vins de Pays d'Oc* wines (Oc is the ancient region of Occitanie) are by far the most important of the *Vins de Pays* wines.

★ ★ ★ ★

Albert Bichot 'Vieilles Vignes' Bourgogne Pinot Noir 2013

AOC BOURGOGNE $18.15 (166959) 12.5% ALC.   XD

Vieilles vignes refers to "old vines." There's no standard definition of "old" in any wine law, but as vines age they produce fewer (but more intensely flavoured) grapes, so producers like to highlight them. The flavours in this pinot are well concentrated and quite complex, and they're complemented by juicy acidity. Dry and lightly tannic, it's a very good choice for mushroom risotto, duck, lamb, and roast turkey.

NOTES

....

....

....

....

★ ★ ★ ★ ½

Antonin Rodet Côtes du Rhône 2013

AOC CÔTES DU RHÔNE $13.95 (8979) 13.5% ALC.   XD

Antonin Rodet started making wine in Burgundy in 1875, and the winery now produces wines under various labels in many other French regions. This côtes du Rhône has a very attractive texture: it's juicy and generous and ideal for food. The flavours have good depth and complexity, and the wine is dry and medium bodied, pitched just right for your meal, especially veal or lamb, but turkey or chicken, too.

NOTES

....

....

....

....

★ ★ ★ ★ ★

Bouchard Père & Fils Beaune du Château Premier Cru 2010

AOC BEAUNE PREMIER CRU $37.25 (325142) 13% ALC.   D

This is a serious and seriously enjoyable pinot noir that delivers plenty of complexity and style. The flavours are many-layered and consistent right through the palate. The spine of acidity is balanced, and the wine is dry to the point of astringent, a texture that carries through to the finish. The tannins are drying and manageable. Drink it with duck and rich poultry dishes such as coq au vin.

NOTES

....

....

....

Bouchard Père & Fils Bourgogne Pinot Noir 2014

★ ★ ★ ★ ½

AOC BOURGOGNE $19.95 (605667) 12.5% ALC. XD

If you're looking for a stylish red to go with turkey and cranberries, roast chicken, baked ham, or summer salads, this pinot noir is an excellent candidate. It's made in the understated style often found in Burgundy. Don't be put off by the light colour; the flavours are nicely concentrated, with quite good complexity. It's dry, with moderate and manageable tannins, and well structured.

NOTES

....
....
....
....

NEW!
★ ★ ★ ★ ½
Chanson 'Réserve du Bastion' Pinot Noir 2013

AOC BOURGOGNE $21.95 (50575) 12.5% ALC. XD

[Vintages Essential] This is a lovely pinot noir that delivers across the board. The fruit is ripe and high-toned, consistent right through the palate and backed by acid that's clean, broad, and fresh enough to give the wine some juiciness. The tannins are there, but not intrusive. This is a very good pinot that's versatile enough to handle grilled salmon, grilled lamb, and coq au vin.

NOTES

....
....
....
....
....

NEW!
★ ★ ★ ★
Château Bel Air 2014

AOC BORDEAUX $13.10 (665430) 12.5% ALC D

This blend of merlot, cabernet franc, and cabernet sauvignon goes well with roasted or grilled red meats. It's a concentrated red that's medium-plus in weight and shows well-defined, ripe fruit flavours right through the palate. The broad seam of acidity is well calibrated to the fruit, and the tannins are drying and approachable.

NOTES

....
....
....
....

NEW!
★ ★ ★ ★ ½

Château Canteloup 2012

AOC MÉDOC $19.85 (420000) 13.5% ALC.   XD

Unlike most wines from the Médoc region, where cabernet sauvignon is the main grape variety, this blend is slightly more merlot (55 percent) than cabernet. It has a generous texture that's soft and attractive while being well balanced by clean, refreshing acidity. The flavours are concentrated but not too forward, and show very good definition and focus. Pair this with red meats for sure, but it's not at all out of place with richer poultry, pork, and vegetarian dishes.

NOTES
....
....
....
....

★ ★ ★ ★

Château de Courteillac 2014

AOC BORDEAUX $13.10 (360552) 13% ALC.   XD

This is a merlot-dominant blend, with cabernet sauvignon in a minor role. It's a solid, well-made red with concentrated flavours, some complexity, and clean, nippy acidity—a good example of what older English people call "claret." Medium bodied and dry with light tannins, it's very versatile with food, and it goes well with many red meat, poultry, and pork dishes.

NOTES
....
....
....
....

★ ★ ★ ★

Château de Gourgazaud 2014

AOC MINERVOIS $13.10 (22384) 13.5% ALC.   XD

This is one of the LCBO's veterans, and it earns its longevity not through inertia but by delivering quality and value, vintage after vintage. The aromas and flavours are fairly intense and complex, and the texture is rich, mouth-filling and slightly tangy. Add medium weight, good balance, and drying tannins and you have a very well-built red that goes well with roasted or grilled red meats.

NOTES
....
....
....
....

Château de Vaugelas 'Le Prieuré' Corbières 2014

★ ★ ★ ★

AOC CORBIERES $13.95 (361691) 13.5% ALC. **XD**

A blend of grenache, syrah, carignan, and mourvèdre, this is full of ripe, concentrated fruit from attack to medium finish. There's good complexity and structure, and the acidity comes through the fruit, lightening its depth and providing a texture that verges on juicy. Medium bodied and easy-going in tannins, it's a good choice for well-seasoned red meats and sausages.

NOTES

....

....

....

Château Pipeau Saint Emilion Grand Cru 2012

★ ★ ★ ★ ★

AOC SAINT EMILION $37.95 (302018) 13% ALC. **XD**
GRAND CRU

[Vintages Essential] This is a blend of 90 percent merlot, and 5 percent each of cabernets sauvignon and franc. From one of Bordeaux's most prestigious appellations, it carries its pedigree well. Look for sculpted fruit that shows focus and definition, fine fruit-acid balance, and well-calibrated supporting acidity. It's framed by supple tannins, and is a great partner for roasted and grilled red meats.

NOTES

....

....

....

....

Château Timberlay 2012

★ ★ ★ ★

AOC BORDEAUX SUPÉRIEUR $16.60 (30072) 13.5% ALC. **XD**

This is a well-made, well-balanced merlot (70 percent), cabernet sauvignon (20 percent), and cabernet franc (10 percent) blend that goes very successfully with roasted and grilled red meats. The flavours are consistent right through the palate, show as much depth as breadth, and they're balanced by clean, refreshing acidity. It's dry, and the tannins are moderate, quite supple, and easily managed.

NOTES

....

....

....

....

NEW!
★★★★ ½
Château Tour Carmail 2011
AOC HAUT-MÉDOC $19.80 (419002) 13% ALC. **D**

Unlike most wines from Haut-Médoc, where cabernet sauvignon is the
dominant grape variety, this is mainly merlot. The flavours are quite dense
and concentrated, with lots of complexity and good structure, and they're
set off by fresh, clean acidity. The tannins are supple and well integrated
and this is a very good choice for grilled or roasted red meats.

NOTES
....
....
....
....

★★★★ ½
David Le Mourre de l'Isle Côtes du Rhône 2012
AOC CÔTES DU RHÔNE $17.60 (387779) 14% ALC. **D**

[Vintages Essential, Kosher] This is a blend of syrah (60 percent), grenache
(30 percent), and mourvèdre (10 percent). It delivers lovely fruit flavours
with real complexity and concentration, and the fruit is well supported
by clean, fresh acidity that makes it so suitable for food. The tannins are
perceptible and slightly gripping, but they're easily manageable. Drink
this with grilled or red meats, with richer pork and poultry, or with
mushroom-dominant dishes.

NOTES
....
....
....

★★★★★
E. Guigal Côtes du Rhône 2011
AOC CÔTES DU RHÔNE $19.95 (259721) 13% ALC. **XD**

[Vintages Essential] The Côtes du Rhône appellation turns out vast
volumes of wine, much of it fairly mediocre, so it's important to know
which producers offer the best quality and value. There's no doubt at all
that this, from one of the most-respected producers in the Rhône Valley,
is one of them. It carries its concentrated flavour with lightness and
elegance, and the tangy texture is stylish. Medium bodied, astringently
dry and moderately tannic, it's an excellent choice for red meats.

NOTES
....
....
....
....

Fat Bastard Merlot 2013

NEW!
★ ★ ★ ★

IGP PAYS D'OC $14.95 (610857) 12.5% ALC. D

This is a pretty nice merlot made in an easy-drinking style. It goes with red meats in general and pairs nicely with casual eats such as burgers and barbecued ribs. There's plenty of ripe fruit flavour here, with a generous, round, fleshy texture, and it's well supported by the soft acidity. The tannins are there, adding a touch of dryness, but they're very relaxed.

NOTES

....

....

....

....

François Labet 'Dame Alix' Côtes du Rhône 2014

★ ★ ★ ★

AOC CÔTES DU RHÔNE $12.95 (630657) 12.5% ALC. D

This is a blend of grenache, syrah, and mourvèdre, three of the classic grapes of this region that spreads across a broad swath east of the River Rhône near the Mediterranean. The wine has quite solid flavours, decent complexity and a slightly tangy texture. It's dry and medium bodied with moderate tannins. Drink it with pasta in tomato sauce or with roast chicken or turkey (with cranberries).

NOTES

....

....

....

Garriotin Malbec 2011

★ ★ ★ ★

AOC CAHORS $13.60 (340927) 12% ALC. D

Argentina has a lock on the most popular malbecs, but it's good to have one from malbec's home in southwest France: Cahors. This shows concentrated fruit with good structure and layering, and clean acidity to lighten everything up. The tannins are moderate, and this is a very good choice when you're having well-seasoned grilled or roasted red meats or a hearty stew.

NOTES

....

....

....

....

....

Georges Duboeuf Brouilly 2014
★★★★

AOC BROUILLY $17.95 (213934) 12.5% ALC.   XD

Brouilly is one of the recognized "Crus" of Beaujolais, the top tier of the region. This one delivers solid and flavourful fruit, with nice complexity, right through the palate, and it's supported by bright and fresh acidity. Try it with a bottle of Beaujolais-Villages (like the one above) to appreciate the difference, and drink both with any of many poultry or pork dishes.

NOTES
....
....
....
....

Gérard Bertrand 'Réserve Spéciale' Cabernet Sauvignon 2014
★★★★

IGP PAYS D'OC $13.95 (234815) 13.5% ALC.   XD

You might think that, coming from the warm South of France, this would be fruit forward and low in acid. But in fact it's a very well-balanced cabernet, with concentrated but by no means overbearing flavours and fresh, clean acidity. The tannins are drying and sleek. It's a very good partner for red meats, but it also goes well with poultry and pork.

NOTES
....
....
....
....
....

Jean-Claude Mas 'Paul Mas Estate' Réserve Cabernet Sauvignon/Merlot 2014
★★★★

IGP PAYS D'OC $13.95 (293134) 14% ALC.   D

Look for well-concentrated, even intense, fruit flavours in this wine. They show good complexity and structure, and they pair well with clean, fresh acidity. It's quite mouth-filling, dense, and fairly smooth with an interesting edge, and the tannins are ripe and drying. This is a very good choice for red-meat dishes and is perfect for well-seasoned grilled steak.

NOTES
....
....
....
....

La Fiole du Pape Châteauneuf-du-Pape

★ ★ ★ ★

AOC CHÂTEAUNEUF-DU-PAPE $39.95 (12286) 13.5% ALC. D

[Non-vintage] You can't miss the bottle. It's gnarled and twisted, with a rough, gritty texture, as if it's been in a fire. But the wine's in very good shape. It's a stylish red that has good structure and food-friendly balance. Look for concentrated flavours with spicy accents and a tangy texture. It's medium bodied and dry, with moderate tannins. Serve it with grilled or roasted red meats.

NOTES

Lavau Côtes du Rhône Villages 2014

NEW!
★ ★ ★ ★ ½

AOC CÔTES DU RHÔNE $13.45 (421024) 13.5% ALC. D
VILLAGES

A fifty-fifty blend of grenache and syrah, this is a lovely red that goes well with red meats, burgers, and charcuterie. The fruit is concentrated and well layered, and it's complemented by a seam of fresh, clean acidity. The tannins are easy-going. This is a dry, medium-weight wine that is generous and substantial but light on its feet. It's priced well for larger gatherings.

NOTES

Les Dauphins Réserve Côtes du Rhône 2014

★ ★ ★ ★

AOC CÔTES DU RHÔNE $13.10 (385385) 13% ALC. D

This grenache-dominant blend is a great choice for grilled or roasted red meats and game, as well as for other hearty dishes prepared in a red wine–based sauce (like coq au vin). The flavours here are concentrated, quite intense even, with good focus and complexity. The acidity is well calibrated to the density of the fruit, and the tannins are drying, with a light grip.

NOTES

Les Jamelles Cabernet Sauvignon 2014

★ ★ ★ ★

VIN DE PAYS D'OC $13.95 (293159) 13% ALC.   **D**

Cabernet sauvignon, one of the main red grapes of Bordeaux, is planted
throughout the world. The vines that produced this are fairly close
to home, in southern France, and they've come up with a style that's
concentrated and well structured in flavour and texture. Look for good
layering, very good acid-fruit balance, and easy-going tannins. It's a
no-brainer for red meats and burgers.

NOTES

....

....

....

....

Louis Bernard Côtes du Rhône Villages 2013

★ ★ ★ ★

AOC CÔTES DU RHÔNE VILLAGES $15.10 (391458) 13% ALC.   **D**

The appellation means that the wine comes from villages within the
Côtes du Rhône that are recognized for making superior wine. This one
is a blend of grenache and syrah, and it delivers lovely flavours that are
focused and consistent right through the palate. Look for a refreshing
texture and easy-going tannins, and drink this with red meats, pork, veal,
and well-seasoned sausages.

NOTES

....

....

....

Louis Jadot 'Combe aux Jacques' Beaujolais-Villages 2012

★ ★ ★ ★

AOC BEAUJOLAIS-VILLAGES $17.95 (365924) 12.5% ALC.   **XD**

[Vintages Essential] Light in tannins, beaujolais (which is made from the
gamay variety) is often a good choice for anyone who finds that red wines
lead to a headache. This one is quite classic: medium bodied and dry with
bright fruit flavours, some complexity, and a vibrant, refreshing texture.
You can serve it slightly chilled, especially in the summer, with roast or
grilled chicken or with roast turkey.

NOTES

....

....

....

....

....

★ ★ ★ ★ ½

Louis Latour Gamay 2013

AOC BOURGOGNE GAMAY $18.15 (361014) 13% ALC. **XD**

It's funny to see a gamay labelled "Bourgogne"—the Duke of Burgundy banished it in the 1300s as a bad, "disloyal" grape variety. It migrated to Beaujolais, where the grapes for this wine came from (Beaujolais is part of Burgundy). This is a lovely wine, full of fresh-but-serious fruit and backed by clean, refreshing acidity. This is quite concentrated; drink it with well-seasoned grilled salmon, pork, and poultry. It's great with turkey.

NOTES

★ ★ ★ ★

Louis Latour Pinot Noir 2012

AOC BOURGOGNE $23.20 (69914) 13% ALC. **D**

This is a reliable red burgundy, now labelled "pinot noir" to help consumers who buy by grape variety, not wine region. It's in one of the classic Burgundy styles: fairly light in colour but with surprising depth and complexity in the flavours, a tangy and refreshing texture, and drying tannins. It's a great choice for roast poultry and cranberries or for grilled salmon.

NOTES

NEW!
★ ★ ★ ★ ½

M. Chapoutier Rasteau 2012

AOC RASTEAU $19.95 (321539) 14% ALC. **D**

Rasteau is one of the villages singled out for producing superior wines within the Côtes du Rhône appellation. Made from grenache and syrah, it has intense aromas and delivers generous and concentrated flavours. The well-calibrated acidity shines through as very attractive juiciness, and the wine, while very dry, is only lightly tannic. It's an excellent choice for braised beef and red meats in general.

NOTES

Mommessin 'Les Épices' Châteauneuf-du-Pape 2013

★ ★ ★ ★

AOC CHÂTEAUNEUF-DU-PAPE $34.35 (42242) 14% ALC. D

Châteauneuf-du-Pape is an iconic appellation in the southern Rhône Valley, near Avignon. The wines can be made from many different varieties, but most, like this one, draw mainly on grenache. Here you'll find richness and complexity of flavour, big body, and real depth to the smooth texture. The tannins are firm but manageable. This calls for food with heft, like grilled game, lamb, or beef.

NOTES

Ogier 'Héritages' Côtes du Rhône 2014

★ ★ ★ ★

AOC CÔTES DU RHÔNE $14.95 (535849) 14% ALC. D

This is a solid and reliable southern Rhône blend of grenache, syrah, and mourvèdre. There's plenty of flavour here, some complexity, and decent structure. It's dry, medium bodied and nicely balanced, with a good tangy texture and moderate tannins. Try it with grilled or roasted red meats, paella, or coq au vin. Each bottle is numbered; mine was 8491.

NOTES

Perrin 'Les Sinards' Châteauneuf-du-Pape 2012

★ ★ ★ ★ ★

AOC CHÂTEAUNEUF-DU-PAPE $36.95 (926626) 13.5% ALC. XD

[Vintages Essential] "Les Sinards" is a sort of junior Château de Beaucastel, an iconic wine from this region, but it surrenders nothing to quality. Made mainly from grenache, with syrah and mourvèdre playing minor roles, this is simply opulent, with fleshy, plush, and layered fruit, finely tuned acidity and supple tannins. From an excellent vintage, this goes well with lamb and other suitably seasoned red meats.

NOTES

Perrin Réserve Côtes du Rhône 2013

★ ★ ★ ★ ★

AOC CÔTES DU RHÔNE $15.95 (363457) 13% ALC. XD

[Vintages Essential] There's tremendous value in this bottle, vintage after vintage. It's a blend of grenache, syrah, mourvèdre, and cinsault, made by the producer of Château de Beaucastel, an iconic wine from Châteauneuf-du-Pape. This côtes du Rhône delivers rich, luscious flavours with an astonishingly intense, smooth, and mouth-filling texture. Dry and well structured with good tannic grip, it's a great choice for grilled or roasted red meats.

NOTES

....

....

....

....

Philippe de Rothschild Merlot 2014

★ ★ ★ ★

IGP PAYS D'OC $12.15 (407544) 13% ALC. XD

The fruit is nicely concentrated and complex, with a core of ripe-sweet fruit. The fruit-acid balance is very good—there's some juiciness in the texture, and are tannins quite firm and gripping. You can ease the tannins with red meat cooked no more than medium rare, and it also goes well with grilled spicy sausages and burgers.

NOTES

....

....

....

....

NEW!

Pisse-Dru Beaujolais 2013

★ ★ ★ ★ ★

AOC BEAUJOLAIS $13.10 (2881) 12% ALC. D

Beaujolais is made from the gamay grape and comes in a range of styles. This is a common enough style, and what makes it attractive is its versatility with food. The fruit is moderate in concentration, but bright and solid right through the palate; the acidity is refreshing, and the tannins negligible. It works with poultry and white fish, grilled salmon, charcuterie, and lighter-flavoured cheeses.

NOTES

....

....

....

Yvon Mau Merlot 2014

IGP VIN DE PAYS DE L'AUDE $10.05 (336743) 12.5% ALC.   D

This is a red you can easily serve at parties and big gatherings where there's a wide range of food; it has the balance, in flavour and fruit-acid relationship, to handle many styles. The flavours are positive but not assertive, the balance is very good, and the tannins are relaxed. It's not too much of anything, but has the right measure of everything.

NOTES

....

....

....

....

....

GERMANY

GERMANY IS FAR BETTER KNOWN for white wine than red, but red wine production is growing far more rapidly, and reds are produced in many of Germany's wine regions. Pinot noir is becoming an increasingly important variety. Because of the cool climate and relatively short growing season, Germany's pinots tend to be in a lighter and crisper style, and they pair easily with food.

Important terms on German wine labels are *Prädikatswein* (the highest-quality classification of wine) and *Qualitätswein* (sometimes followed by *b.A.*, and which designates wines of quality but not of the highest level). Each of these terms is followed by the name of the wine region where the grapes were grown.

Villa Wolf Pinot Noir 2014

★ ★ ★ ★

QUALITÄTSWEIN PFALZ $12.95 (291971) 13% ALC. **D**

Made in a lighter-bodied and dry style, this pinot noir goes well with grilled or roast poultry, roast pork, and grilled salmon, and will pair nicely with many summer salads. The flavours are understated, solid right through the palate and nicely layered, and they are complemented by bright, pleasant acidity.

NOTES

....

....

....

....

GREECE

THE HOT GROWING CONDITIONS in Greece generally make for full-flavoured reds. Although many are produced from native grape varieties, notably agiorgitiko (sometimes called St. George), international varieties such as cabernet sauvignon are also making headway. An AOC-designated wine from Greece (sometimes abbreviated PDO) means that it complies with rigorous laws regulating wine quality. Other wines, referred to as "Regional" (or IGP), are made according to somewhat less stringent laws.

NEW!
★★★★ ½

Alpha Estate 'Axia' Syrah-Xinomavro 2011

IGP FLORINA $17.95 (392282) 14.5% ALC. XD

This fifty-fifty blend from the northwestern part of Greece is a terrific
wine to pair with robust red-meat dishes such as steak, lamb, and hearty
stews, as well as burgers. There's a ton of flavour but it's not a mindless
fruit bomb. It has plenty of complexity and very good structure, and the
tannins are drying but relaxed enough that they add to the pleasure of the
wine.

NOTES
....
....
....
....

★★★★

Boutari Agiorgitiko 2014

PDO MEMEA $13.10 (172148) 12.5% ALC. XD

The agiorgitiko grape variety (also known as St. George) is native to
Greece, and here it makes a wine that goes well with roast chicken, turkey,
and pork, and that easily extends to many burgers and pizzas. It's on the
light side of medium bodied, but delivers well-focused flavours and well-
balanced acidity with easy-going tannins.

NOTES
....
....
....
....

★★★★

Hatzimichalis Cabernet Sauvignon 2009

REGIONAL WINE OF $18.15 (538074) 13.5% ALC. D
ATALANTI VALLEY

This is a quite powerful and very attractive cabernet sauvignon made in
an international style. Look for bold, intense flavours that are echoed in
the big mouth-filling texture. This is a full-bodied cabernet that's dry and
still quite tannic, with a good seam of acidity that suits it for food. Serve it
with grilled red meats, like lamb or beef, that are cooked medium rare at
most and served with lemon wedges.

NOTES
....
....
....
....

Kir-Yianni Paranga 2012

★ ★ ★ ★ ½

IGP MACEDONIA $14.75 (392175) 13.5% ALC.   XD

This is a blend of the Greek xinomavro variety with merlot and syrah. It makes for a full-flavoured red with good complexity and consistency. The acidity is well balanced and the tannins are drying and have a little grip, but are easily manageable. It's a very good choice for grilled red meats (especially lamb) and makes a welcome guest at barbecues where you'll be grilling seasoned sausages and ribs.

NOTES

....

....

....

....

....

Tsantali Rapsani 2011

★ ★ ★ ★

PDO RAPSANI $13.20 (392167) 13% ALC.   XD

A blend of three indigenous Greek grape varieties (xinomavro, krassato, and stavroto), this comes from a region on the lower slopes pf Mount Olympus. It delivers a quite juicy texture and well-layered flavours in the fruit, with the acid coming through in a balanced and fresh way. With moderate tannins, it's a good pairing for pork and poultry, simple red meats, and medium-strength cheeses.

NOTES

....

....

....

....

....

HUNGARY

HUNGARY IS BEST KNOWN INTERNATIONALLY for its sweet wine from the Tokaji district. There are many Hungarian dry red wines, but they have made little impact on the Canadian market. One of the most commonly grown red grape varieties is kékfrankos, but many other varieties are grown.

Jászbery 'Szekszárdi' Kékfrankos 2012

★ ★ ★ ★

AOP SZEKSZÁRDI $9.00 (371583) 12.5% ALC.   D
KÉKFRANKOS

In the old days, I'm told, this wine (from the Szekszárd wine region) was known as "sex on Saturday." Be that as it may, you can drink this any day of the week, and with many different foods, as it swings to red meats and to lighter poultry and pork. Look for bright flavours with a ripe-sweet core that are solid right through the palate, and to a good dose of food-friendly acidity. It's dry (I'd have said XD) with relaxed tannins.

NOTES

....

....

....

....

ITALY

ITALY HAS LONG PRODUCED RED WINES from native grape varieties, but in recent years international varieties like merlot and cabernet sauvignon have also been widely planted. There are many regional varieties, the best known being sangiovese, which is originally from Tuscany but now grown and used in winemaking throughout Italy. Other important varieties are nero d'Avola from Sicily and primitivo from southern Italy.

The highest-quality classification of Italian wines is DOCG *(Denominazione di Origine Controllata e Garantita),* which indicates a wine made to stringent regulations and from a few specified grape varieties. Wines in the next category, DOC *(Denominazione di Origine Controllata),* follow similar rules. Wines labelled IGT *(Indicazione Geografica Tipica)* or IGP *(Indicazione Geografica Protetta)* are made according to less-stringent regulations and may use a wider range of grape varieties. This doesn't mean that a DOCG wine is necessarily better than an IGT/IGP— in fact, some of Italy's most famous wines are IGT/IGP wines. Overall, you'll find quality and value in all these categories, as this list shows.

Ascheri Barbera d'Alba 2012

★ ★ ★ ★ ★

DOC BARBERA D'ALBA $16.05 (219790) 13% ALC.   D

Barbera is a too-little known grape variety. Taste this lovely wine and you'll find that it delivers high-toned and concentrated flavours from start to finish, with a well-tuned texture that's fresh and lively. It's dry with light tannins, and it makes a great partner for many tomato-based Italian dishes (pizza, pasta, meats) as well as for pork, chicken, and turkey dishes.

NOTES
....
....
....
....

Barone Montalto Nero d'Avola/Cabernet Sauvignon 2013

★ ★ ★ ★ ½

IGT SICILIA $9.45 (621151) 13.5% ALC.   D

For a long time, Sicily was better known for white wine than red, but in the last few years the reds, led by the native nero d'Avola grape variety, have been going gangbusters. Nero d'Avola is most of the blend here, and it delivers rich, complex flavours of dark fruit and spice. It's almost full bodied, with a generous and tangy texture. This is pretty big and needs the same kind of food, so pair it with well-seasoned red meat.

NOTES
....
....
....
....
....

Bersano 'Costalunga' Barbera d'Asti 2013

★ ★ ★ ★ ½

DOCG BARBERA D'ASTI $13.10 (348680) 13% ALC.   XD

Made 100 percent from barbera grapes, this is a very versatile wine for food. Try it with burgers and pizza, red meats and poultry, pasta dishes and pork. Barbera is often like that when it's made in this style: dry and medium bodied, with solid, concentrated, and well-defined fruit, but understated rather than forward, with well-balanced acidity and moderate tannins.

NOTES
....
....
....
....

Bolla Amarone della Valpolicella Classico 2010

★ ★ ★ ★ ½ DOC AMARONE DELLA $37.30 (352757) 16% ALC. D
VALPOLICELLA CLASSICO

Amarone often impresses because it is such a big-bodied and deeply flavourful wine. But with the heft you also need what this example offers: complexity, structure, and balance. It's the difference between a wine that kills food and wine that complements it. This has it all, and although the tannins are firm (you could easily keep it until 2018), it's drinking well now. Pair it with well-seasoned red-meat dishes.

NOTES
....
....
....
....
....

Bolla Valpolicella Classico 2014

★ ★ ★ ★ DOC VALPOLICELLA CLASSICO $13.95 (16840) 12% ALC. XD

Valpolicella is a wine region in the Veneto, in northeastern Italy, and all valpolicella wines are red. The most common grape is corvina, an Italian variety, and here it makes for a straightforward and very drinkable wine that's excellent for tomato-based pasta, meat, and vegetable dishes. Look for well-focused fruit flavours and a juicy texture from the supporting acidity.

NOTES
....
....
....

Caparzo Toscana Sangiovese 2012

★ ★ ★ ★ IGT TOSCANA $13.10 (361022) 13% ALC. D

This is a well-made sangiovese that brings to the table the bright acidity and solid fruit that go so well not only with hearty, tomato-based Italian dishes, but also roasted poultry, pork, and red meats in general. The flavours are solid right through, with good complexity, and the balanced acidity adds some juiciness. The tannins are drying and relaxed.

NOTES
....
....
....

Carione Brunello di Montalcino 2010

★ ★ ★ ★ ★

DOCG BRUNELLO DI MONTALCINO $30.25 (266668) 14.5% ALC.   XD

This is a very stylish red and a rare brunello (a clone of sangiovese from the Montalcino region) that's available year round in Ontario. Look for a lot of elegance here, with a texture that's generous, smooth, yet high toned. The flavours are focused and subtly layered, and the tannins are moderate-to-firm, yet supple enough to be manageable. All the components are very well integrated, it goes beautifully with red meats and full-flavoured Italian dishes.

NOTES
....
....
....

Frescobaldi 'CastelGiocondo' Brunello di Montalcino 2011

★ ★ ★ ★ ★

DOCG BRUNELLO DI MONTALCINO $50.95 (650432) 13% ALC.   XD

[Vintages Essential] This elegant, stylish wine is made from sangiovese grapes and aged in barrels for three years. You'll find that the flavours are dense, deep, and broad, with multi-layered complexity and firm tannins. All this is supported by a solid platform of acidity that cuts through the weight of the fruit and makes for a tangy, fresh texture that invites you back to the glass. This is a big wine for big, well-seasoned food.

NOTES
....
....
....

Frescobaldi 'Castiglioni' Chianti 2013

★ ★ ★ ★

DOCG CHIANTI $15.10 (545319) 13% ALC.   D

Made by Frescobaldi, this is an attractive and affordable chianti that shows plenty of flavour and verve. Look for well-defined fruit right through the palate, and a line of bright, fresh acidity that translates into a juicy texture. The tannins are supple and ripe. This is a no-brainer with many Italian dishes, but why not stray geographically and pair it with coq au vin or paella?

NOTES
....
....
....

Cesari Amarone Classico 2011
★ ★ ★ ★ ½

DOC AMARONE DELLA
VALPOLICELLA CLASSICO $38.95 (426718) 14.5% ALC.   D

This has all the structure and defined flavours you expect from a well-made amarone. It's deep and broad, with layers of pungent, vibrant, and mature flavours that come on in waves. The texture is rich, tangy, mouth-filling, and surprisingly lively given the weight of the wine. Dry, full bodied, and delicious, this amarone calls for substantial and well-seasoned red-meat dishes, like a rosemary/garlic rack of lamb or pepper steak.

NOTES

Cesari 'Mara' Valpolicella Ripasso Superiore 2014
★ ★ ★ ★ ½

DOC VALPOLICELLA RIPASSO $18.15 (506519) 13.5% ALC.   D
SUPERIORE

This is a full-bodied, dense red with a mouth-filling, smooth texture that's a good choice when you're grilling well-seasoned red meats, game, or richly flavoured sausages. It has attractive and full-flavoured fruit and good complexity. The tannins are moderate and drying, the acidity is well calibrated to the intensity of the fruit, and there's some distinct juiciness to the texture.

NOTES

Citra Montepulciano d'Abruzzo 2014
★ ★ ★ ★

DOP MONTEPULCIANO $8.35 (446633) 13% ALC.   D
D'ABRUZZO

Like many Italian wine names, this combines a grape variety (montepulciano) and a wine region (Abruzzo). This is a surprisingly well-made and attractive wine for the price. You get rich, concentrated flavours that flow through consistently from start to finish. It might not be all that complex, but the texture—tangy and refreshing—is very appealing, and this is ideal for grilled red meats and hearty tomato-based vegetarian stews. It's also available in a 1.5 L bottle.

NOTES

Citra Sangiovese 2014

★ ★ ★ ★

IGP TERRE DI CHIETI $8.05 (480756) 13% ALC.   **XD**

It's amazing that anyone can grow grapes, make and bottle wine, ship it
from Italy, pay all the mark-ups and taxes, and sell it for eight dollars. And
it's good wine. Here you'll find solid and attractive flavours with decent
complexity, balanced by bright, clean acidity. The tannins are soft. This
is an obvious choice for pizza parties, but don't stop at pizza, when it goes
so well with many pastas, not to mention burgers and grilled seasoned
sausages.

NOTES
....
....
....
....

Colle Secco Montepulciano d'Abruzzo 2011

★ ★ ★ ★

DOP MONTEPULCIANO $9.25 (195826) 13% ALC.   **D**
D'ABRUZZO

This is an unassuming but really lovely red. (The grape is montepulciano
and the region is Abruzzo.) You'll find the flavours are concentrated,
fruity, rich, nicely layered, and fresh, and that the acidity clicks in
effectively. It's dry, more than medium bodied, and very versatile at the
table: try it with pasta, hearty stews, red meats, pork, and rich poultry
dishes, as well as with pizza.

NOTES
....
....
....
....

Costa Mediana Valpolicella Ripasso 2013

★ ★ ★ ★ ½

DOC VALPOLICELLA RIPASSO $16.95 (377648) 13.5% ALC.   **D**

This is an impressive wine. It comes with dense, layered, and defined
flavours that are well structured and consistent right through the palate.
The spine of fresh acidity shines through and lightens the fruit, and the
tannins are moderate and supple. This is a wine for well-seasoned red and
game meats, whether roasted or grilled.

NOTES
....
....
....

Cusumano Nero d'Avola 2014

★ ★ ★ ★

IGT TERRE SICILIANE $13.10 (143164) 14% ALC.   XD

Sicily is coming to the fore with some high-quality and many good-value wines. This is one of the latter, made from the indigenous variety that's become the island's signature grape. Here you get quite intense flavours with limited complexity and good consistency, as well as an attractive tangy texture. With moderate tannins, it's a good bet for well-flavoured red meats and pasta dishes.

NOTES

Dogajolo Toscana Rosso 2014

★ ★ ★ ★

IGT TOSCANA $15.95 (361501) 13.5% ALC.   XD

A blend of 80 percent sangiovese and 20 percent cabernet sauvignon, this is an excellent choice for richer tomato-based dishes like pastas and stews, as the acidity in the wine picks up the acidity in the tomato. But it extends easily to red meats in general, as well as richer pork and poultry dishes. Look for quite vibrant but deep, concentrated, and layered flavours here, with fresh acidity, and tannins that have a gentle grip.

NOTES

Enrico Serafino Barbaresco 2012

★ ★ ★ ★ ★

DOCG BARBARESCO $21.00 (341156) 14% ALC.   D

Made from the nebbiolo variety, barbaresco wines are often serious and seriously enjoyable. This one is no exception. It's bold and stylish, with dense, well-structured fruit that delivers a layered flavour profile from attack to long finish. The acidity is beautifully calibrated, and the tannins are softening and manageable. Drink this with well-seasoned red meats and game.

NOTES

Enzo Vincenzo Ripasso Valpolicella 2013

★ ★ ★ ★

DOC VALPOLICELLA RIPASSO $15.05 (194118) 13.5% ALC. D

Made by the ripasso method (which includes partially dried skins left over from amarone production), this delivers rich, intense flavours with a real line of ripe-sweetness through the palate. The acidity brightens and lightens it, making it good with food, and the tannins are firm but manageable. This is a good choice for hearty red-meat dishes and for meats in hearty, intensely flavoured sauces.

NOTES
....
....
....
....

ERA Montepulciano d'Abruzzo 2014

★ ★ ★ ★

DOC MONTEPULCIANO $9.95 (255844) 13.5% ALC.   D
D'ABRUZZO

There's an attractive acid bite to this wine, the sort of thing that tells you it's going to go well with tomato-based dishes of many kinds, from simple spaghetti bolognese to some gourmet lasagna (as long as it keeps the tomato). The fruit is bright and vibrant and persistent right through, and the tannins are relaxed. This is an organic wine.

NOTES
....
....
....
....

Farina 'Le Pezze' Valpolicella Ripasso Classico Superiore 2013

★ ★ ★ ★ ½

DOC VALPOLICELLA RIPASSO $16.00 (195966) 13.5% ALC.   D
CLASSICO SUPERIORE

The name is a mouthful, and so is the wine. Made in the concentrated ripasso style, this is a versatile red that goes well with many red meats as well as hearty tomato-based stews and pasta dishes. The fruit is focused and slightly high-toned, with depth and complexity. The acidity adds tanginess to the full, generous texture, and the tannins are supple and approachable.

NOTES
....
....
....

Farnese 'Casale Vecchio' Montepulciano d'Abruzzo 2014

★ ★ ★ ★ ½

DOC MONTEPULCIANO $10.95 (612788) 13% ALC. **D**
D'ABRUZZO

This is a very impressive wine, with flavours that are sweet, rich, and dense but well defined, and with good complexity. It's dense and mouth-filling in texture, but the acidity is well integrated and leaves your palate feeling saturated but refreshed. Dry and full bodied, it's a great choice for meat-rich Italian dishes as it is for any red meat or hearty stew.

NOTES

....
....
....
....

Farnese 'Fantini' Sangiovese 2014

★ ★ ★ ★ ½

IGT PUGLIA $8.45 (512327) 12.5% ALC. **D**

This is a well-made red that shows the hallmarks of sangiovese. Look for bright acidity, which is a key feature that makes this wine so good with food. The acidity supports lovely flavours that are nicely concentrated and show decent complexity. The tannins are easy-going, and everything is in balance here. It's great with pizza, tomato-based pastas, and many red meat and poultry dishes.

NOTES

....
....
....
....

Farnese 'Fantini' Negroamaro 2014

★ ★ ★ ★

IGT PUGLIA $8.95 (143735) 13.5% ALC. **D**

Negroamaro ("black bitter") is a variety indigenous to Puglia, in the south of Italy, where this wine comes from. Despite the name, this wine is deep red (not black) and full of sweet and ripe (not bitter) flavours. It has very good acidity, is dry with easy-going tannins and is a great choice for casual meals of pasta, burgers, and many red meats.

NOTES

....
....
....
....

Folonari Valpolicella Ripasso Classico Superiore 2013

DOC VALPOLICELLA RIPASSO $18.15 (481838) 13.5% ALC.   **D**
CLASSICO SUPERIORE

To make a ripasso wine, the wine is fermented on the skins left over from making amarone, which itself is made from dried grapes. This gives ripasso wines more depth and complexity, and you can taste and feel the effects here. There's very good concentration, lots of complexity, firm and drying tannins, and very good acidity. This is an excellent choice for hearty Italian food.

NOTES
....
....
....
....

★ ★ ★ ★ ½

Fontanafredda Barolo 2011

DOCG BAROLO $29.95 (20214) 14% ALC.   **D**

This is a gorgeous wine, one of those winners that combines power and depth with elegance and style. The fruit flavours are concentrated and nicely structured, and they're complemented by refreshing and well-calibrated acidity. The tannins are firm and ripe, and the wine is a great choice if you're having osso bucco or any meat in a tomato-based sauce.

NOTES
....
....
....

★ ★ ★ ★ ½

Fontanafredda 'Briccotondo' Barbera 2014

DOC PIEMONTE $14.95 (372987) 13.5% ALC.   **D**

Barbera is a variety that deserves to be more popular. Take this example, which delivers great flavours that are layered and serious but also fresh and vibrant. The acidity is pitched right—forward and juicy but not at all harsh—and the tannins are drying, but in the background. It's a perfect wine for mushroom risotto or any tomato-based Italian dish.

NOTES
....
....
....
....
....

THE 500 BEST-VALUE WINES IN THE LCBO | 2017

ITALY | RED WINES

Gabbiano Chianti 2014

★ ★ ★ ★

DOCG CHIANTI $14.10 (78006) 12% ALC. **XD**

The grapes for this dry, medium-weight wine are from the estate of
the Castello di Gabbiano, a thirteenth-century castle located on a hill
in chianti classico country. In the bottle you'll find attractive flavours
that are solid, fresh, and concentrated, with good complexity. They're
complemented by a tangy and refreshing texture and great balance. This
goes very well with a rich, tomato-based pasta or any stew in a red wine
and tomato sauce.

NOTES

Gabbiano Chianti Classico 2013

★ ★ ★ ★ ★

DOCG CHIANTI CLASSICO $18.15 (219808) 13% ALC. **D**

"Classico" means that the grapes for the wine came from the area that
was originally demarcated for chianti; it has been expanded over time.
This example delivers lovely rich and focused flavours with impressive
complexity and range. They're complemented and supported by fresh
acidity that gives a sleek and refreshing texture, and framed by supple
tannins. Drink it with classic Italian dishes.

NOTES

Il Sestante 'I Pianti' Ripasso Valpolicella 2013

★ ★ ★ ★ ½

DOC VALPOLICELLA $18.95 (267070) 13% ALC. **D**
RIPASSO SUPERIORE

This is a very attractive and well-priced ripasso valpolicella that
demonstrates the intensity the ripasso method contributes. The fruit is
concentrated, well structured, and nicely focused, and the acidity shines
through with juicy freshness. The tannins are sweet and drying, and it's a
great choice for poultry, pork, and the usual Italian gastronomic suspects.

NOTES

Illuminati 'Riparosso' Montepulciano d'Abruzzo 2014

★ ★ ★ ★ ½

DOC MONTEPULCIANO $14.10 (269985) 13.5% ALC.   **D**
D'ABRUZZO

Made 100 percent from the montepulciano grape variety, this is a delicious wine you can drink with pizza, and many red-meat dishes. The flavours are full of ripe-sweet fruit that is complex and quite sleek in texture, and they're accompanied by lovely fresh acidity that makes you want to drink another glass. It's dry, with fine-grained, ripe tannins, and all the components are very well integrated.

NOTES
....
....
....
....

Leonardo Chianti 2014

★ ★ ★ ★

DOC CHIANTI $16.00 (372391) 12.5% ALC.   **D**

This one of the rare chiantis still packaged in the straw basket (*fiasco,* in Italian) that chiantis used to be as a matter of course. It has retro value for older wine drinkers, who in the 1960s might have drunk the wine, then turned the bottle into a wax-covered candle-holder. The wine inside today is bright and vibrant in flavour and texture, medium weight, and a perfect pairing for a nostalgic dinner of spaghetti bolognese with meatballs.

NOTES
....
....
....
....

Luccarelli Primitivo 2014

★ ★ ★ ★

IGP PUGLIA $10.95 (253856) 13.5% ALC.   **D**

Less expensive primitivo—the variety now associated with the southern region of Puglia—can be intense and heavy. This one achieves real lightness of being and brings a juicy texture without sacrificing the concentration of flavour. It's very attractive and, more important, very drinkable wine, and goes well with many tomato-based dishes as well as poultry and pork.

NOTES
....
....
....

RED WINES | ITALY

NEW!
★ ★ ★ ★ ½

Marchesi di Barolo Barolo 2010

DOCG BAROLO $39.95 (168179) 14.5% ALC.   D

This is a robust, full-bodied red from a highly regarded region of
Piedmont. Barolo is considered by some people to be the pinnacle of
Italian wine, and this is a very good example. The flavours are rich and
dense, but well structured and impressively complex, while the acidity
shines through, clean and fresh. The tannins are well integrated. This is a
great choice for classic Italian meat-based cuisine.

NOTES

....
....
....

NEW!
★ ★ ★ ★ ½

Masi Bonacosta Valpolicella Classico 2014

DOC VALPOLICELLA CLASSICO $16.65 (285585) 12% ALC.   D

Here's more evidence you can have relatively low alcohol in a good quality
wine—the level of alcohol that was common not so long ago. Look for
concentrated and high-toned flavours here. They are focused and well
defined and backed by a good level of acidity. The tannins keep it dry and
it's a great choice for hearty pastas, charcuterie, and many red meats.

NOTES

....
....
....
....
....

★ ★ ★ ★ ★

Masi Campofiorin 2012

IGT ROSSO VERONA $21.20 (155051) 13% ALC.   XD

Campofiorin is a stylish wine that's reliable year after year. It's made by
adding freshly fermented wine to the grape skins that remain after the
super-rich amarone is made. The result has dense, intense flavours of
complex, ripe fruit. It's more than medium bodied, and dry with a tangy
texture. It's a real treat to drink and goes well with spicy pasta dishes with
grated Parmigiano Reggiano.

NOTES

....
....
....
....
....

Masi 'Costasera' Amarone della Valpolicella Classico 2010

★ ★ ★ ★ ½

DOC AMARONE DELLA
VALPOLICELLA CLASSICO

$42.45 (317057) 15% ALC. **D**

Amarone is made from grapes that are allowed to dry on bamboo mats for a few months before being pressed. The drying process leads to more concentrated flavours and complexity, as this wine shows. Its layers of ripe and mature fruit are dense and well focused, and it has an opulent texture. Dry and moderately tannic with a tangy texture, it's an excellent choice for rich red-meat dishes and aged hard cheeses.

NOTES

....
....
....
....

Masi 'Modello delle Venezie' Rosso 2015

★ ★ ★ ★ ½

IGT DELLE VENEZIE

$13.10 (533026) 12% ALC. **D**

Made mainly from the refosco and merlot grape varieties, this is a lovely wine made in a modern style. It's sleek-textured and shows full-on flavours that are focused, sculpted, and layered. The acidity is nicely calibrated, and the tannins are light to moderate. It's terrific with many Italian meat dishes (think osso buco), and goes well with red meats generally.

NOTES

....
....
....
....

Matervitae Negroamaro 2013

★ ★ ★ ★

IGT PUGLIA

$8.65 (254300) 13% ALC. **D**

The meaning of "amaro" in the grape name is disputed. Most agree that "amaro" means "bitter," but producers of the variety would rather think that it comes from the Greek word for "black." It doesn't matter, as the wine isn't bitter. This one is fruity and concentrated, a little rustic in a positive way, and the fruit-acid balance is very good. Drink it with burgers, ribs, and well-seasoned sausages, or with red meats generally.

NOTES

....
....
....
....

Mauro 'Alberello' Primitivo del Salentino 2014

NEW!
★ ★ ★ ★

IGT PRIMITIVO DEL SALENTINO $11.60 (441790) 13.5% ALC.   D

Like many Italian wines, this couples a grape variety (primitivo, known in California as zinfandel) to a region (Salentino, in the heel of the Italian boot). Although primitivo originated in Croatia, it is made in a distinctive style in Italy. You'll find bright, solid, serious fruit here, underpinned by clean and quite vibrant acidity. The tannins dry it out but they're largely unobtrusive. Drink it with spicy or well-seasoned lamb, beef, pork, and poultry dishes.

NOTES

Monna Lisa Chianti Classico 2013

NEW!
★ ★ ★ ★

DOCG CHIANTI CLASSICO $15.30 (378133) 13% ALC.   XD

"Chianti Classico" refers to the region that more or less corresponds to the territory originally defined for chianti wine; since then it has expanded considerably. This wine, made from grapes grown in the region, shows food-friendly juiciness in its texture, the result of the interplay of the ripe, concentrated fruit and a broad seam of fresh acid. With moderate tannins, this is a very good choice for hearty Italian dishes featuring meat or mushrooms.

NOTES

Monte Antico 2011

★ ★ ★ ★ ½

IGT TOSCANA $15.95 (69377) 13% ALC.   XD

[Vintages Essential] This delicious wine is a blend of sangiovese—the signature red grape variety of Italy—merlot, and cabernet sauvignon. It delivers robust and concentrated flavours that show complexity and depth, and a plush, full texture that's refreshing and tangy. A hint of rusticity adds to its attractiveness. This is an excellent wine for full-bodied Italian dishes, and it extends equally well to other rich meat and vegetarian cuisines.

NOTES

Montezovo 'Sa' Solin' Valpolicella Ripasso 2013

★ ★ ★ ★

DOC VALPOLICELLA RIPASSO $17.95 (650713) 13.5% ALC.   XD

Made from a blend of indigenous grapes, this is a weighty red in terms of flavour; the fruit is concentrated and quite deeply textured, with persistence right through the palate. The acidity lightens the wine, with clean juiciness, and the tannic frame is moderate and manageable. Drink this with hearty Italian meat dishes, with braised lamb, and with well-seasoned beef.

NOTES

....

....

....

....

Montresor Amarone della Valpolicella 2012

★ ★ ★ ★ ½

DOCG AMARONE DELLA $36.35 (240416) 15% ALC.   D
VALPOLICELLA

Made from three grape varieties (50 percent corvina and 25 percent each of rondinella and molinara), this delivers the intensity and style you expect of an amarone. Look for concentrated, well-layered fruit that has both breadth and depth, complemented by a broad seam of clean, fresh acidity. The fruit is ripe-sweet and framed by supple tannins. It's an intensely flavoured wine that needs the same sort of food, so think of well-seasoned red meats and game.

NOTES

....

....

....

....

Negrar Valpolicella 2014

★ ★ ★ ★

DOC VALPOLICELLA $13.95 (74963) 12% ALC.   D

[1 L bottle] This is a well-made red in a format that's ideal for gatherings where you're serving pizzas, burgers, grilled sausages, red meats, pork, or poultry. It's one of those well-priced, inexpensive, workhorse reds. Look for bright flavours with a decent level of complexity and concentration, clean and refreshing acidity, and easy-going tannins.

NOTES

....

....

....

Oggi Primitivo 2014

★ ★ ★ ★

IGT SALENTO $8.85 (86421) 13% ALC.   D

Primitivo is the same grape variety as California's zinfandel. This example shows concentrated flavours that are solid right through the palate, nicely structured, and well balanced with the acidity that clicks in and cuts through the ripe-sweet fruit. The tannins are drying and add a little more complexity. Drink this with red meats, including richer dishes like braised lamb shanks or well-seasoned beef.

NOTES

....

....

....

....

Pasqua Passimento 2013

★ ★ ★ ★ ½

IGT VENETO $13.95 (141952) 14% ALC.   D

The *appassimento* method of drying grapes before pressing them (to concentrate flavours) is used for amarone, but is being more and more widely employed. This example, made from corvine, croatina, and merlot, is rich in flavour and big and generous in body. But it has the right degree of acidity to let you enjoy more than one glass (or two). Pair it with substance foods, like well-seasoned red meats.

NOTES

....

....

....

....

Rocca delle Macìe Chianti Classico 2013

★ ★ ★ ★ ½

DOCG CHIANTI CLASSICO $18.95 (741769) 13.5% ALC.   XD

[Vintages Essential] This is a long-time favourite chianti classico (the "classico" meaning the grapes came from the original Chianti region, which has been expanded over time). It's quite a young chianti, with bight and vibrant flavours and a lively texture, and you can hold it a few years. Dry and medium bodied, it goes well with Italian tomato-based dishes, whether pasta, meat, or pizza.

NOTES

....

....

....

....

Rocca delle Macìe Chianti Riserva 2011

★ ★ ★ ★ ½

DOCG CHIANTI CLASSICO $15.95 (111641) 13.9% ALC.   **XD**

[Vintages Essential] To qualify for Riserva status, a chianti must be aged much longer than a non-Riserva, in barrel and bottle, before being released for sale. Think of it as pre-cellared. This one delivers very attractive flavours with complexity and consistency, with a dose of bright acidity and drying tannins. It's a great choice for many pastas and other dishes prepared in a tomato-based sauce.

NOTES

....
....
....
....
....

Rocca delle Macìe 'Vernaiolo' Chianti 2014

★ ★ ★ ★ ½

DOCG CHIANTI $14.95 (269589) 12.5% ALC.   **D**

The Chianti wine region produces tens of millions of bottles of wine a year, some of it exquisite, some of it not. (If you're old enough to have been drinking chianti in the 1960s and 1970s, you'll remember some of the not-exquisite chiantis in wicker baskets.) Vernaiolo is an attractive chianti with quite concentrated flavours of ripe fruit. It's dry, moderately tannic, juicy textured, and perfect with chicken parmesan.

NOTES

....
....
....

Ruffino 'Aziano' Chianti Classico 2014

★ ★ ★ ★ ½

DOCG CHIANTI CLASSICO $18.15 (307025) 13% ALC.   **XD**

This is a very attractive chianti, a blend that's mostly (minimum 80 percent) sangiovese, with merlot and cabernet sauvignon playing bit (but important) parts. You'll find the fruit both serious and bright, with good complexity and range, while the well-measured acid contributes some juiciness to the texture. The tannins have a relaxed grip, and this is a great choice for meats Italian-style.

NOTES

....
....
....
....

★ ★ ★ ★ ½

Ruffino Il Ducale Sangiovese-Syrah-Merlot 2012
IGT TOSCANA $20.20 (27797) 13% ALC.   XD

It might seem an unlikely blend for Tuscany, where sangiovese is king, but producers have been working other varieties into blends with it for decades. This is a very good example (about half sangiovese and a quarter each of syrah and merlot), with vibrant but serious fruit, refreshing acidity, and moderate tannins. It holds together very well, and is a great choice for hearty stews and red meats cooked Italian-style.

NOTES

★ ★ ★ ★ ★

Ruffino 'Riserva Ducale' Chianti Classico Riserva 2012
DOCG CHIANTI CLASSICO $24.95 (45195) 13% ALC.   D
RISERVA

This is a very stylish chianti from the original (Chianti Classico) zone of production. Look for ripe fruit flavours that have breadth, depth, definition, and focus, and are consistent from start to long finish. They're harnessed to a broad seam of fresh acidity that shines through the fruit. With ripe tannins and a juicy texture, it's a great choice for steak Florentine, osso bucco, and braised lamb.

NOTES

NEW!
★ ★ ★ ★

Sartori Valpolicella Classico 2014
DOC VALPOLICELLA CLASSICO $13.95 (378109) 12.5% ALC.   D

This is a nicely made red that goes well with richer pasta dishes and stews with a tomato base, such as chicken cacciatore. You'll find the flavours well layered and characterised by high-toned notes that are complemented by quite vibrant acidity. The tannins dry the wine out a little, but they're essentially quite relaxed. All the components—fruit, acid, alcohol, and tannins—are very well integrated.

NOTES

Sella & Mosca Riserva Cannonau di Sardegna 2011

DOC CANNONAU DI
SARDEGNA
$16.95 (425488) 13.5% ALC. XD

[Vintages Essential] Cannonau is the Sardinian name for the variety the French call "grenache" and the Spanish call "garnacha," and it grows very successfully on this Mediterranean island. This is a robust, full-flavoured red with just a hint of attractive rusticity in the texture. The fruit is layered, the acid balance is very good, and the tannins are moderate and manageable. It's an excellent partner for osso buco or for many lamb or other red-meat dishes.

NOTES

....

....

....

....

NEW!
★ ★ ★ ★ ½

Tedeschi Amarone 2011

DOCG AMARONE DELLA
VALPOLICELLA
$42.95 (433417) 15.4% ALC. D

[Vintages Essential] Amarone is one of the richest and most robust Italian wines and it's highly valued for its intensity and suitability for well-seasoned, rich dishes of various kinds. This very good example delivers the classic style: great concentration of flavour, with layered complexity and very good structure, clean acidity that cuts through the density of the fruit, and supple, well-integrated tannins.

NOTES

....

....

....

★ ★ ★ ★

Tini Sangiovese di Romagna 2013

DOC SANGIOVESE DI ROMAGNA $7.75 (179432) 12% ALC. XD

At this price, you can't go wrong with this wine when you're gathering friends for pizza or a meal of pasta. Made from sangiovese in the region of Romagna, it's a dry red with a texture that's concentrated and bright. The freshness of the acidity shows through nicely and complements the vibrant flavours, which are modestly complex but consistent from start to finish.

NOTES

....

....

....

★ ★ ★ ★ ★ **Tommasi Ripasso Valpolicella Classico Superiore 2012**

DOC VALPOLICELLA RIPASSO $22.95 (910430) 13% ALC. **D**
CLASSICO SUPERIORE

[Vintages Essential] This terrific valpolicella is a great choice for many hearty Italian-style dishes with a tomato base, as well as for well-seasoned poultry and pork. The fruit is serious but vibrant, well-defined and consistent, and its weight is lifted by clean and fresh acidity. The tannins are ripe and slightly gripping. In all, it's an impressive and versatile red.

NOTES
....
....
....
....

★ ★ ★ ★ ★ **Umberto Fiore Barbaresco 2012**

DOCG BARBARESCO $18.30 (254870) 14% ALC. **XD**

Made from nebbiolo grapes in an appellation near Barbaresco in the region of Piedmont, this is a beautiful wine, characterized by poise and style. Already more than four years old, it shows slightly maturing fruit flavours that are still lively and fresh, with vibrant acidity and drying tannins. It's medium bodied and a perfect choice for roast poultry, grilled duck, and many medium- to strong-flavoured mature cheeses.

NOTES
....
....
....
....

★ ★ ★ ★ **Valpantena Valpolicella 2014**

DOC VALPOLICELLA $13.05 (377556) 13% ALC. **D**

Made from a blend of indigenous Italian grapes, this is a fairly robust, medium-to-full-bodied red that goes well with a range of foods, from hearty tomato-based pasta, to pizzas, burgers, red meats, and pork. Look for well-layered flavours right through the palate, a good dose of fresh and clean acidity, and tannins that are drying and have a light grip.

NOTES
....
....
....
....

★★★★★

Villa Annaberta Amarone della Valpolicella 2012

DOCG AMARONE DELLA
VALPOLICELLA
$38.95 (433961) 15% ALC. **D**

This is a delicious amarone made in the classic style. You'll find gorgeous fruit displaying depth as well as breadth, layered complexity, and impressive length. The structure is very good, as is the acid-fruit balance, while the tannins are nicely integrated. You can cellar this to the end of the decade or drink it now with richly flavoured red meats, pastas, and cheeses.

NOTES

....

....

....

....

★★★★ ½

Villa Annaberta Valpolicella Ripasso Superiore 2013

DOC VALPOLICELLA RIPASSO $16.95 (378091) 14.5% ALC. **D**

Look for a lot of complexity in the multi-layered, dark flavours of this full-bodied wine. They give you a generous clue to the sort of food it needs: weighty and full-flavoured, meaning you think of grilled red meats and game or flavourful wild mushroom–based dishes. For all the weight of the wine, the acidity plays a lighter game, making it food friendly, while the tannins dry it out nicely.

NOTES

....

....

....

....

....

THE 500 BEST-VALUE WINES IN THE LCBO | 2017

MEXICO

WINE PRODUCTION IN MEXICO dates back to the early 1500s, when Spanish settlers tried to grow grapes in the area now occupied by Mexico City. Over time, more suitable regions were identified in the north, and Mexico's main wine region is now in Baja California, not far from the border with the US.

Mexican wine producers draw on a wide range of grape varieties.

L.A. Cetto Petite Sirah 2013

VALLE DE GUADALUPE, $12.25 (983742) 14% ALC.   XD
BAJA CALIFORNIA

[Vintages Essential] This is a very well-priced full-fruit red wine that transcends Mexican cuisine and goes well with many gringo red-meat dishes. Look for layered and concentrated flavours right through the palate. They're paired with good acidity that makes the wine tangy and edgy. The tannins are moderate, ripe and drying, but easily managed.

NOTES

....

....

....

....

NEW ZEALAND

NEW ZEALAND IS BEST KNOWN for its white wine, especially sauvignon blancs from the Marlborough region in the South Island. But it produces many very good red wines, too, including merlots from the North Island. It's the pinot noirs that are especially impressive, notably from Central Otago (the southern-most wine region in the world) and Marlborough, two regions in the South Island. Most are made in volumes too small for the LCBO, but we are seeing a better selection every year.

Kim Crawford Pinot Noir 2014

★ ★ ★ ★ ½

SOUTH ISLAND $19.95 (626390) 13.5% ALC. **XD**

[Vintages Essential] The South Island includes two important pinot noir regions, Marlborough and Central Otago, so this could be sourced by both. It's a soft-textured, very approachable wine that's restrained rather than exuberant (like many NZ pinots). You'll find the fruit concentrated and layered, with just the right dose of acidity and easy-going tannins. Drink it with grille sausages, roast turkey, and charcuterie.

NOTES

....

....

....

....

Matua Pinot Noir 2013

★ ★ ★ ★ ★

MARLBOROUGH $18.15 (358952) 13% ALC. **D**

This is a really lovely pinot noir that delivers balance, poise, and elegance. The flavours are neither assertive nor understated, but are concentrated, focused, and well structured. The spine of acidity is broad and fresh, adding juiciness to the texture, and the tannins are ripe and supple. You can cool this down a little—10 minutes in the fridge will do it—and then enjoy it with grilled salmon, pork, or poultry.

NOTES

....

....

....

....

NEW!

★ ★ ★ ★ ½

Stoneleigh Pinot Noir 2014

MARLBOROUGH $18.95 (54353) 14% ALC **D**

This is a juicy textured pinot from a region too often associated only with sauvignon blanc. The flavours are positive, well-defined, and high-toned, and they're supported by fresh acidity that pops on the attack and follows right through the palate. The tannins are supple and integrated and this is a great partner for grilled salmon and tomato-based dishes of all kinds (whether featuring meat or not).

NOTES

....

....

....

....

Villa Maria 'Private Bin' Pinot Noir 2013

★ ★ ★ ★

MARLBOROUGH $19.95 (146548) 13.5% ALC.   **XD**

Pinot noir is a popular wine partly because it's versatile with food.
Depending on style, it goes well with red meats, poultry, pork, many
vegetarian dishes, and some fish and seafood. This example shows intense
flavours with some sweet notes, good complexity, and the right acidity
to make it juicy. Try it with roast duck or turkey, grilled salmon, or
mushroom risotto.

NOTES

....

....

....

....

ONTARIO

THE MOST SUCCESSFUL RED GRAPE VARIETIES in Ontario are those that thrive in its cool climate, specifically gamay, pinot noir, and cabernet franc. The best known of Ontario's three wine regions is Niagara Peninsula (which is now divided into a number of sub-regions, such as Twenty Mile Bench and Niagara Escarpment). Prince Edward County is also represented in this list.

Wine labelled VQA (Vintners Quality Alliance) followed by a region is made from grapes grown in that region. The VQA classification also means that the wine has been tested and tasted by a panel. VQA wines from Ontario can be made only from grapes grown in Ontario.

Most non-VQA wines in the Ontario section of the LCBO are blends of a small proportion of Ontario and foreign wine. They are not included in this book because the range varies greatly from year to year, depending on the Ontario grape harvest.

Cave Spring Cabernet/Merlot 2013

★★★★ ½

VQA NIAGARA ESCARPMENT $15.95 (407270) 13% ALC.   **XD**

This is a lovely red blend that shows well-focused, sleek fruit from start to finish. There's the merest hint of greenness that adds an interesting and positive note to the flavours, and the fruit-acid balance is right on—clean and juicy. This is a great choice for red-meat dishes, but has the versatility to extend to pork and poultry as well.

NOTES

....

....

....

....

Cave Spring Gamay 2014

★★★★ ½

VQA NIAGARA ESCARPMENT $15.95 (228569) 13% ALC.   **D**

Gamay grapes grow very successfully in the Niagara Peninsula, but it's a variety overlooked by too many wine drinkers. This one from Cave Spring is just lovely. It has bright flavours of fresh fruit, and very refreshing, clean acidity. It's dry and medium bodied, and the juiciness in the texture makes you want to eat. Drink it with roast chicken or baked ham. I like to serve it just slightly chilled.

NOTES

....

....

....

....

....

Cave Spring Pinot Noir 2014

★★★★ ½

VQA NIAGARA ESCARPMENT $18.95 (417642) 12% ALC.   **XD**

Cave Spring built its reputation on riesling, but it fires on all varietal cylinders. This is a really fine-tasting pinot noir. Look for vibrant, well-layered fruit, a very clean and refreshing texture, and drying but easy-going tannins. It's dry and medium bodied and an excellent match for roast turkey or chicken, poached salmon, or a tomato-based vegetarian dish.

NOTES

....

....

....

....

NEW!
★ ★ ★ ★ ★

Château des Charmes Cabernet Franc 2013

VQA NIAGARA-ON-THE-LAKE $14.95 (162602) 13% ALC. **XD**

This is a lovely cabernet franc made in an easy-drinking, popular style without conceding any of the character typically associated with the variety. The flavours are well defined and nicely layered, and the fruit is well supported by clean acidity. The tannins are light to moderate, drying, but easily manageable, and this is a good partner for many red meats, as well as for richer poultry dishes, such as coq au vin.

NOTES

....

....

....

NEW!
★ ★ ★ ★

Château des Charmes Cabernet Sauvignon 2014

VQA NIAGARA-ON-THE-LAKE $14.95 (370320) 13.5% ALC. **D**

There's a very attractive edginess to this cabernet. It shows in the texture, which is quite juicy, thanks to bright, clean acidity, and in the flavours, which are focused and well layered, with as much depth as breadth. The tannins are almost moderate, and they dry the wine out effectively, but they're not intrusive. I like it. It's a good pairing with red meats in general, but has the acidity for hearty tomato-based dishes of many kinds.

NOTES

....

....

....

....

★ ★ ★ ★ ½

Château des Charmes Gamay Noir 2014

VQA NIAGARA-ON-THE-LAKE $13.95 (57349) 12.8% ALC. **XD**

Gamay (or gamay noir) is the grape variety used to make beaujolais, but this wine is more substantial than most generic beaujolais, and is another wine that makes the case that gamay deserves to be Ontario's signature red grape variety. What you get are concentrated flavours enlivened by a food-friendly and very refreshing texture. It's medium bodied and dry, and it goes extremely well with roast turkey and cranberries, as well as chicken, pork, and many pastas.

NOTES

....

....

....

....

NEW!
★★★★ ½

Château des Charmes Pinot Noir 2014

VQA NIAGARA-ON-THE-LAKE $14.95 (454967) 13% ALC.   XD

This is a slightly fuller-bodied pinot than many from Niagara, but it in no way detracts from its quality. The fruit is concentrated and focused, with good depth, and it's underpinned by clean, refreshing acidity. The tannins are ripe and drying, but essentially relaxed, and everything is well integrated. Drink it with red meats such as veal and lamb, though it also extends to chicken and turkey. For a non-meat dish, think of mushroom risotto.

NOTES

★★★★

Coyote's Run Five Mile Red 2014

VQA NIAGARA PENINSULA $16.95 (283416) 12.5% ALC.   D

This blend of cabernet (55 percent), merlot (35 percent), pinot noir (8 percent), and syrah (2 percent) is attractive, easy drinking, and very versatile with food. It's medium weight and dry with light tannins, and the flavours are solid all the way through. With bright and refreshing acidity, this goes well with turkey, chicken, and pork, but it also extends to roasted and grilled red meats.

NOTES

★★★★

Coyote's Run Pinot Noir 2014

VQA NIAGARA PENINSULA $19.95 (53090) 12.5% ALC.   XD

This is a pinot noir in a mid-range style that delivers plenty of defined and complex flavours. The acidity is spot-on and contributes some juiciness to the texture, while the tannins dry the wine out and are quite easy-going. It goes very well with chicken, turkey, and grilled salmon, and will extend to many lighter red-meat dishes.

NOTES

EastDell Gamay Noir 2013

NEW!
★ ★ ★ ★

VQA NIAGARA PENINSULA $13.95 (214890) 12.5% ALC D

This is a pretty astringent gamay, making it less suitable for drinking alone but a very good choice for the table. I would happily drink it with salmon, chicken, pork, and many kinds of salads. The fruit is quite plump and round, with a little fruit-sweetness that complements the overall dryness. There's decent complexity and the acid is clean and effective.

NOTES
....
....
....
....
....

Featherstone Cabernet Franc 2014

NEW!
★ ★ ★ ★ ½

VQA NIAGARA PENINSULA $19.20 (64618) 12.3% ALC. XD

[Vintages Essential] Cabernet franc does very well in the Niagara region, and this is a very successful example. The flavours are classic franc: high toned, bright, layered, ang fresh. They're complemented by clean, fresh acidity, giving a juicy texture that sets the wine up for food. Drink it with grilled salmon, lamb, pork, and with red meats generally. The tannins are drying and easily manageable.

NOTES
....
....
....
....

Flat Rock Cellars Pinot Noir 2013

NEW!
★ ★ ★ ★ ½

VQA TWENTY MILE BENCH $20.20 (1545) 13% ALC. XD

[Vintages Essential] This is a lovely pinot noir that combines real approachability with structure and complexity. It makes drinking quality pinot noir a pleasure, even for consumers who tend toward easy-drinking styles. The flavours are positive, lifted, and well defined, and the acidity shines through, giving the texture a rounded edge. It's very versatile with food. Try it with pork, poultry, lamb, and grilled salmon.

NOTES
....
....
....
....

Foreign Affair 'The Conspiracy' Red 2013

★ ★ ★ ★ ★

VQA NIAGARA PENINSULA $19.95 (149237) 12.8% ALC.   D

[Vintages Essential] This is a delicious blend of cabernets sauvignon and franc and merlot, refermented on appassimento skins. The flavours are rich, sweet-cored, and forward, but well modulated and structured, showing deep complexity. The acidity is spot-on; it freshens the wine and adds some juiciness, and the tannins are drying and approachable. Pair this with grilled meats where sauces or condiments add a touch of sweetness.

NOTES

....

....

....

....

Grange of Prince Edward Estate Pinot Noir 2012

★ ★ ★ ★

VQA PRINCE EDWARD COUNTY $19.20 (230227) 13% ALC.   XD

This pinot noir, on the light side of medium weight, delivers nicely layered, high-toned fruit right through the palate. It's supported by a seam of vibrant acidity that contributes freshness and food-friendly juiciness to the texture. It's very dry, almost astringent, and the tannins are supple and drying. It's an excellent choice for many poultry and pork dishes, and for grilled salmon.

NOTES

....

....

....

....

NEW!

Henry of Pelham 'Old Vines' Baco Noir 2014

★ ★ ★ ★ ½

VQA ONTARIO $19.95 (459966) 14% ALC   D

The "old vines" referred to here were planted by the Speck family (owners of Henry of Pelham) in the 1980s and 1990s. Older vines generally bear less fruit, but grapes with more intensity, and you can sense that here in the dense and deep flavours that show plenty of layered nuances. It's well structured and balanced and goes very well with rich, full-flavoured meals such as game, lamb, steak, and many pizzas.

NOTES

....

....

....

Henry of Pelham Pinot Noir 2013

★ ★ ★ ★ ½

VQA NIAGARA PENINSULA $16.95 (13904) 12.5% ALC.   XD

Henry of Pelham is one of Niagara's mid-size quality wineries, run by the affable Speck brothers (three of them). With great balance between the fruit and acidity, this attractive pinot noir makes a successful partner for grilled lamb, veal chops, or well-herbed roast chicken. It's medium bodied, with attractive and vibrant flavours and a juicy, refreshing texture.

NOTES

....

....

....

....

NEW!
★ ★ ★ ★ ½
Hidden Bench Estate Pinot Noir 2013

VQA BEAMSVILLLE BENCH $29.95 (274753) 13.6% ALC.   XD

[Vintages Essential] This is a serious but very drinkable pinot noir from one of Niagara's outstanding wineries. You'll find very good depth of flavour here, along with plenty of complexity and structure, while the fresh, clean acidity clicks in to give the fairly rich texture some food-friendly juiciness. It's very dry (there's some tannic grip) and it's a very good choice for duck, goose, and lamb. This is a wine you can drink now or age a few years.

NOTES

....

....

....

....

★ ★ ★ ★
Inniskillin Pinot Noir 2014

VQA NIAGARA PENINSULA $15.95 (261099) 12.2% ALC.   D

This is a lighter and more vibrant style of pinot noir that I would rate **XD** (Extra-Dry) rather than **D** (Dry). It shows fruit that's quite complex, defined, and consistent from start to finish, and the acidity shows through assertively, giving the wine some juiciness and an almost astringent texture. It's a very good choice for roast or grilled chicken and pork, and will go very well with grilled Atlantic salmon.

NOTES

....

....

....

....

NEW!
★ ★ ★ ★

Jackson-Triggs Reserve Cabernet Franc/Cabernet Sauvignon 2014

VQA NIAGARA PENINSULA $13.95 (560680) 12.8% ALC. D

Look for a mouth-filling, soft texture here, as the fruit develops over the palate. It's concentrated and well defined, and supported by gentle acidity. The tannins are drying and the wine verges on astringency in the finish. This is an obvious choice for many red-meat dishes, not to mention barbecue favourites such as burgers and ribs. But you can also serve it up with well-flavoured cheeses.

NOTES
....
....
....
....

NEW!
★ ★ ★ ★ ★

Malivoire Gamay 2013

VQA NIAGARA PENINSULA $17.95 (591313) 13% ALC. D

[Vintages Essential] The gamay variety does very well in Ontario, and this is a fine example. It has the high-toned flavour and texture of a well-made gamay from optimal grapes. You'll find it full of fresh flavour backed by fresh, clean acidity in perfect balance, with supple tannic dryness. It's a great partner for grilled salmon, poultry, and pork.

NOTES
....
....
....
....

NEW!
★ ★ ★ ★ ½

Malivoire 'Guilty Men' Red 2014

VQA NIAGARA PENINSULA $15.95 (192674) 12.5% ALC. D

A blend of cabernet sauvignon (48 percent), merlot (25 percent), cabernet franc, gamay, and pinot noir, this is a delicious, high-toned red that goes well with duck, lamb, mushroom risotto, and grilled spicy sausages. The flavours are positive and consistent right through, and the clean, vibrant acidity makes for a juicy texture. The tannins are supple and easy-going.

NOTES
....
....
....
....

NEW!
★ ★ ★ ★ ½

Megalomaniac 'Homegrown' Red 2013

VQA NIAGARA PENINSULA $15.95 (260364) 13% ALC.   D

This is a bright and juicy red blend that carries the weight of its fruit lightly. There's a lot of concentration here, but the clean acidity makes it refreshing and the sort of wine you can pair with many different food styles from red meats to poultry, from pizza to burgers. It's very dry (the tannins are well integrated, with just a hint of grip) and medium bodied.

NOTES

....

....

....

....

....

★ ★ ★ ★ ½

Megalomaniac 'Pompous' Cabernet-Merlot 2013

VQA NIAGARA PENINSULA $15.95 (341610) 13% ALC.   D

The back label explains the name. Inside the bottle you get a nicely pitched blend that delivers consistently focused fruit through the palate, with some ripe-sweetness at the core. The fruit-acid balance is very good, with some juiciness in the texture, and the tannins are drying and easy-going. You can drink this with red meats, but it easily accommodates pork and poultry too.

NOTES

....

....

....

....

NEW!
★ ★ ★ ★

Peninsula Ridge Merlot 2014

VQA NIAGARA PENINSULA $14.95 (61101) 13.1% ALC.   XD

Cool-climate merlot is often very attractive, as it delivers more acidity than many merlots show. Here the acidity comes through as a tangy texture, verging on juicy, giving the wine the edge it needs to be food-versatile. With flavours that are concentrated and decently complex, this merlot makes a very good partner for red meats, burgers, and stews (meat or vegetarian), as well as for pork and poultry.

NOTES

....

....

....

....

Rosehall Run 'Defiant' Pinot Noir 2014

★ ★ ★ ★ ½

VQA ONTARIO $18.95 (307769) 12.5% ALC.   D

This is a pinot with verve and lively brightness. The fruit is solid and well-defined, and although the wine is well balanced, it's as if the acidity is the active ingredient, giving the wine a vibrant and juicy texture. It's a wine that calls for food, and it goes well with poultry, pork, grilled salmon, and beet salad.

NOTES

....

....

....

....

....

Southbrook 'Connect' Organic Red 2014

★ ★ ★ ★ ½

VQA ONTARIO $17.95 (249565) 12.9% ALC.   XD

This is an impressive red from one of Niagara's more stunning wineries. It's organic and made from 50 percent cabernet franc, a quarter each of zweigelt and gamay, and a touch of merlot. Look for a refreshing texture that supports fruit that's ripe, focused, and quite complex. It's dry, with moderate tannins, and goes well with red meats, pork, and hearty vegetarian or vegan dishes.

NOTES

....

....

....

....

Southbrook 'Triomphe' Cabernet Sauvignon 2014

★ ★ ★ ★ ½

VQA NIAGARA PENINSULA $22.95 (193573) 12.6% ALC.   XD

[Vintages Essential] This is a very well-made cabernet that shows remarkable concentration and ripeness for a cool Niagara vintage. Look for well-defined and nuanced flavours and acidity that's bright, fresh, and well calibrated. The tannins are drying, slightly grippy, but very manageable. Drink it with red meats generally, but it also goes well with pork and some poultry dishes.

NOTES

....

....

....

....

★ ★ ★ ★

Strewn 'Cottage Block' Merlot 2013

VQA NIAGARA PENINSULA $14.95 (303149) 13% ALC.   D

Cool-climate merlot generally offers acidity with a bit more bite than its warm-climate cousins, and is that much more amicable when faced with food. This is a nice example, where the understated fruit meet clean, fresh acidity to make a well-measured red that's versatile at the table. Drink it with poultry and pork, with grilled salmon, or with simple red-meat dishes.

NOTES

....

....

....

★ ★ ★ ★

Sue-Ann Staff 'Fancy Farm Girl' Flamboyant Red 2012

VQA NIAGARA PENINSULA $14.95 (394080) 11.5% ALC.   D

The back label explains the name. Inside the bottle you get a nicely pitched blend that delivers consistently focused fruit through the palate, with some ripe-sweetness at the core. The fruit-acid balance is very good, with some juiciness in the texture, and the tannins are drying and easy-going. You can drink this with red meats, but it easily accommodates pork and poultry too.

NOTES

....

....

....

....

NEW!
★ ★ ★ ★

Thirteenth Street 'Burger Blend' Red 2014

VQA NIAGARA PENINSULA $14.95 (419945) 13.5% ALC.   XD

A lot of popular wines are named for meat, and too many of them are unbalanced, big-fruit-low-acid efforts that swamp most of the food they get near. This an exception—a gamay and pinot noir blend that delivers plenty of fruit flavour, to be sure, but also good balance and a juicy texture. It's designed to be drunk with burgers, of course, but comes in myriad styles and forms (try yours with a slice of beet), and goes as well with ribs and red meats generally.

NOTES

....

....

....

★ ★ ★ ★

Union Red 2010

VQA NIAGARA PENINSULA $13.95 (197152) 12.5% ALC.   D

This is an interesting blend of merlot, cabernet, gamay, and pinot noir.
It delivers plenty of fruit and you'll find a core of sweetness with good
complexity. The acidity is clean and fresh, and the tannins are light to
moderate; they certainly dry the wine out at the end. This is a good bet for
many red meats, and it extends to pork and richer poultry dishes too.

NOTES

....

....

....

....

★ ★ ★ ★

Vineland Estates Cabernet Franc 2013

VQA NIAGARA PENINSULA $14.95 (594127) 12% ALC.   XD

This juicy cabernet franc is full of bright fruit flavours that are ripe,
focused, complex, and persistent from start to finish. The acidity shines
through cleanly and refreshingly, and the tannins are drying but with
negligible grip. You can drink this with many red-meat dishes, but it's
flexible enough to encompass chicken and pork.

NOTES

....

....

....

....

....

THE 500 BEST-VALUE WINES IN THE LCBO | 2017

OREGON

OREGON IS A SIGNIFICANT producer of red wine, and is well known for its pinot noirs. The Willamette Valley is the main wine-producing area.

Amity Pinot Noir 2013

★ ★ ★ ★

WILLAMETTE VALLEY $28.80 (124594) 13% ALC.   D

This is a very attractive pinot noir in a well-paced mid-weight style. The fruit is high-toned and consistent from juicy attack to decent finish, and it's complemented by well-calibrated acidity that ensures the juiciness persists. The tannins are well integrated, and this is a fine choice for roasted or grilled poultry or pork, or for grilled Atlantic salmon.

NOTES

....

....

....

....

RED WINES

PORTUGAL

PORTUGAL IS BEST KNOWN FOR PORT, and it seems logical that some of its best red wines are made from grape varieties permitted in port. They tend to be full of flavour, assertive in texture, and quite big bodied. This also means that Portuguese reds are mainly made from indigenous grapes, and producers have generally resisted planting international varieties such as cabernet sauvignon and syrah. Portugal is a good source for inexpensive reds, as the following list shows.

The name of a region following DOC *(Denominação de Origem Controlada)* signifies a designated Portuguese wine region.

★ ★ ★ ★   **Catedral Reserva Dão 2012**

DOC DÃO $10.95 (219816) 13% ALC.   **D**

There's plenty of flavour and a quite rich texture in this affordable blend of alfrocheiro, tinta roriz and touriga nacional, all grape varieties permitted in the making of port. The fruit-acid balance is good and there's a decent degree of complexity and light tannins. Dry and more than medium bodied, it's a very good choice for well-seasoned, grilled, and roasted red meats.

NOTES

★ ★ ★ ★   **Delaforce Tinto 2012**

DOC DOURO $13.35 (332585) 13.5% ALC.   **XD**

This is a blend of three grape varieties (touriga nacional and franca, with tinta roriz), drawn from vines with an average age of 45 years. Vine age contributes to the concentration of the fruit flavours, and this wine shows it clearly. There's good depth and layering, along with structure and the balance you need for food. It's dry and moderately tannic, and pairs well with red meats and hearty mushroom dishes.

NOTES

★ ★ ★ ★   **Foral Douro 2012**

DOC DOURO $9.05 (239046) 13.5% ALC.   **XD**

This is another of the well-priced, hearty reds that Portugal produces. Made from the tinta roriz, barroca, and touriga franca varieties, this very dry red shows an attractive, young rusticity, and makes you think of grilled spicy sausages and barbecued red meats. The flavours are concentrated and generous, the acidity is properly balanced, the tannins are drying, and the texture is tangy and bright.

NOTES

★ ★ ★ ★

JP Azeitão Tinto/Red 2014

VINO REGIONAL DE
PENINSULA DE SETDBAL

$9.05 (286195) 13.5% ALC. **D**

Made from two indigenous grape varieties plus syrah, this is a robust and slightly rustic red that's perfect for get-togethers when you're grilling sausages, ribs, or hamburgers. The flavours are concentrated with decent complexity, the acidity is fresh, and the tannins are drying and relaxed.

NOTES

....

....

....

....

★ ★ ★ ★

Periquita Original 2014

VINHO REGIONAL DE
PENINSULA DE SETDBAL

$9.05 (25262) 13% ALC **XD**

Portugal turns out not only many higher-priced quality wines (some of which are in Vintages) but also many good, less-expensive wines like this. It's a three-way blend that delivers plenty of flavour, some complexity, and good fruit-acid balance. You can't go wrong opening it with a burger, grilled seasoned and spicy sausages, or a hearty pizza.

NOTES

....

....

....

....

★ ★ ★ ★ ½

Pessoa da Vinha Reserva Touriga National 2013

DOC DOURO

$12.80 (370411) 14% ALC. **XD**

Here's a chance to try a 100 percent touriga nacional, one of Portugal's best indigenous grape varieties. It has its own character, but think of cabernet sauvignon. Like cab, this example of touriga nacional delivers plenty of complex flavour, good structure and balance, and fairly firm tannins. It's built for red meats and hearty dishes, so pair it with grilled steaks, burgers, and seasoned sausages.

NOTES

....

....

....

....

SOUTH AFRICA

MOST OF THE WINE REGIONS OF SOUTH AFRICA are warm, and this tends to make for reds that have concentrated flavours and fairly high alcohol. The conditions are right for a wide range of grape varieties. The country's signature red grape is pinotage, a cross of two varieties that was developed there in the 1920s. More popular varieties found in the LCBO are shiraz, merlot, and cabernet sauvignon.

Wines from official South African wine regions are called Wines of Origin. In this list, the letters WO followed by a region indicate where the wine is from.

Big Oak Red 2014

★ ★ ★ ★

WO WESTERN CAPE $12.10 (350595) 14% ALC.   D

This blend of shiraz and cabernet sauvignon is made by Bellingham, a reliable South African producer. Don't worry, this is not a big, oaky wine; it's named for the tree in the garden of the winery's founders. It's an easy-drinking, well-balanced blend that shows quite deep flavours and some complexity, through and through, and it's an easy choice when you're having a crowd for a barbecue.

NOTES

....
....
....
....

Cathedral Cellar Cabernet Sauvignon 2012

★ ★ ★ ★ ½

WO WESTERN CAPE $15.95 (328567) 13.5% ALC.   XD

[Vintages Essential] This is a quite impressive cabernet sauvignon, packed with plenty of fruit and flavour complexity, with the added assets of structure and balance. The weight of the fruit is offset by judiciously calibrated acidity, making it easy to drink and great with food. It's a natural choice for grilled red meats, whether steak or hamburgers, or anything in between.

NOTES

....
....
....
....

NEW!
★ ★ ★ ★

Fleur du Cap 'Bergkelder Selection' Cabernet Sauvignon 2013

WO WESTERN CAPE $12.95 (457101) 14% ALC.   XD

This is new in the LCBO—another cabernet sauvignon, it's true, but a cut above many at this price. Look for nicely modulated flavours that deliver complexity and structure, together with well-calibrated acidity that freshens the fairly concentrated fruit. The balance is very good and the tannins relaxed. Drink it with well-seasoned meats and hearty vegetarian dishes, or with fairly strong-flavoured cheeses.

NOTES

....
....
....
....

★ ★ ★ ★   **Goats do Roam Red 2014**

WO WESTERN CAPE $12.95 (718940) 14% ALC.   **XD**

The story goes that the winery's goats got into the vineyards and ate the best and tastiest fruit. Sounds like they have a great future as consultants. It's also a play on words for the Côtes du Rhône grape varieties (syrah, cinsault, mourvèdre, carignan, grenache) used in the blend. This is consistently well made, vintage after vintage, with defined flavours and excellent balance. Drink it with red meats, pork, and poultry.

NOTES
....
....
....
....
....

★ ★ ★ ★   **Nederburg 'Winemaster's Reserve' Shiraz 2013**

WO WESTERN CAPE $12.10 (527457) 14.5% ALC.   **XD**

The striking characteristic of this dry, medium-weight shiraz is its balance. You'll find all the concentrated fruit flavours you expect from the variety but, unlike many at this price that are fruity and flat, the texture here is juicy and refreshing. That means it goes especially well with food, and it's versatile enough to handle red meats, veal, pork, and poultry.

NOTES
....
....
....
....
....

★ ★ ★ ★ ½   **Porcupine Ridge Syrah 2014**

WO SWARTLAND $14.95 (595280) 13.5% ALC.   **XD**

[Vintages Essential] This is an impressive syrah in a distinctly New World style, with plenty of fruit up front, but it carries its weight well and delivers effectively in terms of balance and structure. The dense, dark, spicy flavours are reined in by fresh acidity, and the tannins are drying. This is made for red meat, so drink it with well-seasoned steak or lamb.

NOTES
....
....
....
....

Roodeberg Red 2014
NEW!
★ ★ ★ ★

WO WESTERN CAPE $12.60 (7187) 14% ALC. XD

There's a good level of complexity in this blend, which one page on the company website says is "the winemaker's secret," and another reveals it's 43 percent cabernet sauvignon with shiraz, merlot, petit verdot, tannat, cabernet franc, and "2 percent other." Whatever. It's a full-flavoured, dry, balanced wine with refreshing acidity, and it's an easy choice for red meats, grilled sausages, burgers, and other informal dishes.

NOTES
....
....
....
....

The Wolftrap Syrah/Mourvèdre/Viognier 2014
★ ★ ★ ★ ½

WO WESTERN CAPE $13.95 (292557) 14.5% ALC. D

Made by prestigious South African producer Boekenhoutskloof, this is a delicious blend that's a natural for grilled, well-seasoned red meats. It's dry and well balanced with rich, dark fruit flavours that show very good layered complexity. The acidity comes through effectively, keeping it fresh and drinkable, and the tannins are ripe and slightly gripping, but very manageable.

NOTES
....
....
....
....

Thelema Mountain Red 2013
★ ★ ★ ★

WO WESTERN CAPE $13.15 (222570) 14.5% ALC. D

This is a blend of shiraz, petit verdot, cabernet sauvignon, grenache, and cabernet franc. Did I forget anything? More to the point, did they? But it's a successful blend that delivers plenty of layered flavours, good depth and definition, and effective backing by a broad seam of clean, fresh acidity. It's an easy choice for red meats, and will extend to pork and rich poultry dishes.

NOTES
....
....
....
....

SPAIN

SPAIN IS WELL KNOWN for its red wines. Among the many wine regions, Rioja is probably the most recognizable, but you'll find reds from a number of others on this list. Tempranillo is Spain's signature grape variety, but wine is made from many other native and international varieties, as this selection shows.

The initials DO *(Denominación de Origen)* indicate a wine from one of Spain's designated wine regions. Two of them, Rioja and Priorat, have been elevated to a higher level: DOC *(Denominación de Origen Calificada)*. Wines labelled VDT *(Vino de la Tierra)* are quality regional wines made to less rigorous criteria.

Antaño Reserva Rioja 2009

NEW!
★★★★★

DOC RIOJA $16.85 (427369) 13.5% ALC. XD

Several years older than most wines in the LCBO, this comes to you pre-cellared. There are definitely some mature notes in the flavours, but the fruit is still quite fresh and the wine itself is refreshing and clean, thanks to the very good acid-fruit balance. The tannins are drying and mostly integrated, and this makes a very good partner for roasted or grilled game and red meats.

NOTES

Beronia 'Elaboración Especial' Tempranillo Rioja 2013

NEW!
★★★★

DOC RIOJA $16.15 (426981) 14% ALC. XD

This is a very juicy textured tempranillo that's an excellent choice for many lighter red meats and poultry, as well as for meat and vegetarian dishes prepared with a tomato base. The flavours are quite concentrated and well layered, the acid is clean and bright, and the tannins are moderate and drying, but manageable.

NOTES

Beronia Rioja Tempranillo 2012

★★★★

DOC RIOJA $12.95 (243055) 14% ALC. XD

Tempranillo is Spain and Rioja's signature red grape. Here it makes a high-toned wine with bright, concentrated, and reasonably complex fruit, underpinned by a seam of clean, fresh acidity. The tannins are drying and moderate. This is a good choice for simple red-meat dishes, as well as for roast or grilled pork.

NOTES

★★★★ ½ **Beronia Reserva Rioja 2011**

DOC RIOJA $20.95 (50203) 14% ALC. **XD**

This blend of tempranillo, graciano, and mazuelo spent 20 months of its more than six years in French and American barrels. The wine is a really sweet number, too. It's quite elegant in its smooth texture and complex flavour profile, which displays remarkable freshness for its age. The acidity is right-on—balanced and refreshing—and the tannins are fine and supple. Enjoy it with red meats, pork, and many paellas.

NOTES
....
....
....
....

★★★★ ½ **Campo Viejo Rioja Reserva 2010**

DOC RIOJA $17.95 (137810) 13.5% ALC. **XD**

Unlike a generic rioja, a rioja reserva has to age for a specified number of years in barrel and bottle before going on sale. For that reason, reservas tend to have more intensity and complexity . . . as this one does. It delivers quite intense and complex flavours, a rich and tangy texture, and good tannic structure. Medium bodied and dry, it goes well with grilled or roasted red meats or with meat cooked in red wine.

NOTES
....
....
....
....

NEW!
★★★★ ½ **Candidato Tempranillo/Garnacha 2012**

VDT DE CASTILLA $7.65 (523811) 13% ALC. **XD**

A blend of two Spanish varieties (garnacha is called grenache in most of the rest of the world), this is a very well-balanced red that goes as well with poultry and pork as it does with red meats. The flavours are solid and somewhat high-toned, and they're complemented by fresh, clean acidity. It's been aged in small barrels of the kind used in Bordeaux, but the fruit remains pure and bright.

NOTES
....
....
....

Castaño 'La Casona de Castaño' Monastrell 2014

★ ★ ★ ★

DO YECLA $10.05 (143743) 13.5% ALC. **D**

Monstrell (also known as mourvèdre) is the signature grape variety of the Spanish wine region Yecla. Here it makes a flavourful and quite concentrated wine that shows decent complexity and very good fruit-acid balance. It's dry, with relaxed tannins, and pairs easily with burgers, red meats, and hearty stews.

NOTES

....

....

....

....

Castillo de Almansa Reserva 2012

★ ★ ★ ★

DO ALMANSA $13.10 (270363) 14% ALC. **D**

Almansa is a small wine region not far inland from Spain's Mediterranean coast, where the days get very hot during the growing season. It shows in this wine, which has concentrated and quite complex flavours of sweet fruit. It's bone dry and medium bodied, with firm tannins and a tangy texture. It goes very nicely with well-seasoned red-meat dishes all year round, and with hearty stews in winter.

NOTES

....

....

....

....

Castillo de Monséran Garnacha 2013

★ ★ ★ ★

DO CARIÑENA $9.95 (73395) 12.5% ALC. **XD**

This is a basic red that's well priced and great for drinking on the patio when you're serving burgers, ribs, and other well-seasoned red meats. Made from the grape variety better known as grenache, it delivers rich and intense sweet fruit flavours with limited complexity, along with a tangy texture. It's medium bodied and negligibly tannic.

NOTES

....

....

....

....

....

Finca Hispaña Castrijo Rioja Crianza 2011

NEW!
★ ★ ★ ★ ½

DOC RIOJA $13.55 (428359) 13.5% ALC.   D

The front label of each bottle in this series features a photograph of the winemaker, a nice touch that personalizes the wine. This wine, made from tempranillo, is quite robust, with concentrated flavours and plenty of complexity. It shows very good structure and balance, and goes very well with red-meat dishes of many kinds.

NOTES
....
....
....
....

Franco Españolas 'Bordón' Gran Reserva Rioja 2005

NEW!
★ ★ ★ ★ ★

DOC RIOJA $23.25 (428060) 13.5% ALC.   XD

When this book was published, this wine was already 11 years old. Call it pre-cellared. Call it anything, but grab a bottle while this vintage is still on the shelves. It's remarkably fresh, given its age. There are some mature notes, but the fruit is generally fresh and the acidity is bright and clean. The tannins are fully integrated. Drink it with red meats, mushroom risotto, and other hearty dishes.

NOTES
....
....
....
....

Gran Feudo Reserva 2009

★ ★ ★ ★ ½

DO NAVARRA $16.95 (479014) 12.5% ALC.   XD

[Vintages Essential] Made from tempranillo, Spain's signature grape variety, and cabernet sauvignon and merlot, this very attractive dry red goes well with all kinds of grilled red meat, as well as hearty stews and risottos whether or not they feature meat. The fruit is ripe and sweet with layered complexity, and it's underpinned by refreshing acidity and framed by moderate tannins.

NOTES
....
....
....
....

Hécula Monstrell 2013

★★★★½

DO YECLA $10.45 (300673) 14% ALC. XD

This is 100 percent monastrell, which is known under many aliases including mourvèdre and mataró. Monastrell is the signature grape of Yecla, the wine region this is from, and this version is concentrated and full-flavoured, with the fruit held in check by fresh, clean acidity. The tannins are easy-going and this very well-made wine is great with hearty risottos, red meats, and stews.

NOTES

....

....

....

....

Honoro Vera Garnacha 2014

NEW!
★★★★

DO CALATAYUD $12.95 (440867) 14.5% ALC. D

Tempranillo is Spain's signature red grape variety, but garnacha (grenache) runs a good second. This is a robust example with fairly high but well-managed alcohol. The fruit is up-front and assertive, and it's well layered and nicely structured. The broad seam of acidity supports and lightens the fruit, while the tannins are supple and integrated. This is ideal for hearty red-meat dishes, whether they're in the form of steak, ribs, or burgers.

NOTES

....

....

....

....

Hoya de Cadenas Reserva Tempranillo 2011

★★★★

DO UTIEL-REQUENA $12.10 (620989) 12.5% ALC. XD

The appellation is little known (it's near Valencia), but the grape variety is famous; it's Spain's signature grape and the basis for wines from Rioja. Here it's made in a straightforward, uncomplicated style, with plenty of solid fruit that's consistent from start to finish. It's nicely integrated with the acidity and has a tangy texture that pairs well with pork, veal, rich pasta dishes, and many risottos.

NOTES

....

....

....

....

LAN Crianza Rioja 2011

NEW!
★ ★ ★ ★ ★

DOC RIOJA $15.95 (166538) 13.5% ALC. XD

This is a lovely Rioja in which the impressive components are very well integrated. The fruit is optimally ripe, well defined, and complex, and it's complemented by a broad seam of fresh, clean acidity that animates the wine. The tannins are moderate but very approachable. This is a terrific pairing for charcuterie, rich poultry, and pork, and for many red-meat dishes.

NOTES
....
....
....
....

Marqués de Riscal Reserva Rioja 2012

★ ★ ★ ★ ½

DOC RIOJA $24.75 (32656) 14% ALC. XD

Made mainly from the tempranillo variety, with assistance from graciano and mazuelo, this is aged more than two years in oak barrels, and a number more in the bottle, before you can buy it. It's one of the older vintages in the LCBO, and it shows ripe, bright, and maturing flavours with fresh acidity and moderate, drying tannins. It's a good choice for paella, red meats, pork, and many older, full-flavoured cheeses.

NOTES
....
....
....
....

Montecillo Reserva Rioja 2010

★ ★ ★ ★ ½

DOC RIOJA $17.95 (621003) 13.5% ALC. D

This is a lovely example of a reserva rioja—aged for a minimum time in barrel and bottle and not sold until four years after vintage. Look for elegance across the board here, with concentrated and layered flavours, very good balance, and a smooth, attractive texture. Drink it with red meats, well-seasoned poultry, or aged, full-flavour cheeses such as manchego.

NOTES
....
....
....
....

Muga Reserva Rioja 2011

★ ★ ★ ★ ★

DOC RIOJA $23.95 (177345) 13% ALC.   XD

[Vintages Essential] Muga is an iconic name in Spanish wine, and
vintage after vintage this rioja is excellent value. It's a blend that is mostly
tempranillo (70 percent) and grenache (20 percent), and it delivers
wonderful flavours that are concentrated, focused, and layered with
complexity. It's very dry and moderately tannic, but the well-calibrated
acidity gives it the freshness wine needs to pair successfully with food.
Drink it with grilled red meats and hearty stews.

NOTES

....

....

....

....

Solaz Tempranillo/Cabernet Sauvignon 2013

★ ★ ★ ★

VDT DE CASTILLA $11.65 (610188) 13.5% ALC.   D

This medium-weight blend of Spain's signature grape and the ubiquitous
cabernet sauvignon is a good choice for many red-meat dishes, but it's
light enough to handle flavourful chicken (think coq au vin), roast
duck, and goose. The flavours are concentrated and quite high-toned,
and they're supported by a seam of crisp, clean acidity. The tannins are
easy-going.

NOTES

....

....

....

....

Torres 'Sangre de Toro' Garnacha 2014

★ ★ ★ ★

DO CATALUNYA $12.95 (6585) 13.5% ALC.   XD

Garnacha is better known by its French name, grenache, and it's widely
grown in Spain. This is a very good example, delivering plenty of
concentrated flavours right through the palate, with good complexity
and structure. The acidity is clean and refreshing, and the tannins lightly
gripping. It goes well with red meats, but is also friendly to pork, poultry,
and rabbit.

NOTES

....

....

....

Torres 'Gran Coronas' Reserva Cabernet Sauvignon 2011

★ ★ ★ ★ ★

DO PENEDÈS $19.95 (36483) 13.5% ALC. **D**

[Vintages Essential] Torres is one of the best-known names in Spanish wine, and this cabernet sauvignon (with a little tempranillo blended in to give it some Spanish blood) shows the quality and value that underlie its reputation. The fruit is sweet, ripe, layered, and concentrated, and the texture is generous and tangy. It's medium to full in body, dry, and it has a good tannic grip. Enjoy it with grilled or braised red meats.

NOTES

....

....

....

....

Torres Infinite Rojo 2013

★ ★ ★ ★ ½

DO CATALUNYA $13.05 (231795) 13.5% ALC. **XD**

Mostly (85 percent) tempranillo, with the rest cabernet sauvignon, this is an attractive red that goes well with red meats, pork, rich poultry (like coq au vin), and many paellas. It's quite rich and smooth textured, with concentrated flavours that are consistent right through the palate. Dry and medium weight, it shows very manageable and drying tannins.

NOTES

....

....

....

....

WASHINGTON

WASHINGTON STATE IS WELL KNOWN for its reds, particularly merlots from the Columbia Valley region. Like other US states, with the obvious exception of California, it is seldom represented on the LCBO's shelves, although the number of Washington wines there is increasing.

★ ★ ★ ★

14 Hands 'Hot to Trot' Red Blend 2013

COLUMBIA VALLEY $15.95 (226522) 13.5% ALC. **D**

Named for the wild horses that used to live in the hills of Washington State, this blend brings together merlot, syrah, and cabernet sauvignon, with a dash of mourvèdre and some other red varieties. It's intensely flavoured with good layered complexity, and it has a nice seam of clean acidity to keep the fruit honest. It's a very good choice for red meats, as well as burgers and ribs.

NOTES

....

....

....

....

★ ★ ★ ★

Charles & Charles 'Post No. 35' Cabernet Sauvignon & Syrah 2014

COLUMBIA VALLEY $17.95 (363838) 13.5% ALC. **XD**

This is a big-bodied blend that's 68 percent cabernet and 32 percent syrah. Both varieties are represented well in the flavours, which are concentrated, deep, and well layered, and which hold true from start to long finish. The acidity is balanced and the tannins are easy-going. This is a hefty wine that calls for hefty food, so bring it a plate of grilled red meat, ribs, or well-seasoned sausages.

NOTES

....

....

....

....

NEW!
★ ★ ★ ★ ½

Columbia Crest 'Grand Estates' Cabernet Sauvignon 2013

COLUMBIA VALLEY $17.95 (460154) 13.5% ALC. **D**

This is a very attractive cabernet that delivers a juicy texture, layers of ripe fruit, exemplary fruit-acid balance, and sheer drinkability. It was aged in a mix of French and American barrels (25 percent new) and there's a hint of it on the nose and palate, but this is essentially all quality fruit right through the palate. It's a classic style of cabernet that goes with the classic dishes: lamb, other red meats, and game.

NOTES

....

....

....

Columbia Crest 'Grand Estates' Merlot 2013

★ ★ ★ ★ ½

COLUMBIA VALLEY $17.95 (454835) 13.5% ALC.   D

Don't underestimate merlot in its many styles. The variety took a hit in the pinot noir-centred movie *Sideways,* and it's time someone did a merlot-lovers' movie that knocks the many mediocre and overrated pinots out there. That off my chest, this is a rich, plush-textured merlot in the best New World style. Look for smoothness, structure, balance, and complexity, then drink it with grilled or roasted red meats or gourmet burgers.

NOTES

Columbia Crest 'H3' Cabernet Sauvignon 2014

★ ★ ★ ★ ½

HORSE HEAVEN HILLS $19.95 (210047) 14.5% ALC.   D

Another Washington wine with equine associations. Horse Heaven Hills is a designated wine region (called an American Viticultural Area in the US) that's part of the Columbia Valley. This is a really lovely cabernet that shows the depth and concentration of fruit and structure you want of the variety, but is remarkably light on its feet (or hoofs). This is food friendly to the core; pair it with roasted or grilled red meats.

NOTES

ROSÉS

ROSÉ WINES HAVE ENJOYED A RENAISSANCE in the last couple of years—they account for nearly a third of all the wines now drunk in France, for example. Until recently, too many rosés were sweet and simple—fine for everyday drinking but not particularly complex or interesting. Things have changed and rosé has become a popular style, leading producers to make more and more that are well balanced and structured. There are more dry rosés now, along with well-made sweeter styles, and producers have begun to label them by grape variety, as they do for whites and reds.

Beginning in spring, the LCBO releases a large number of rosés for the warm months, when demand is highest. But rosés make good drinking all year round.

Cave Spring Rosé 2015

★ ★ ★ ★

VQA NIAGARA ESCARPMENT $15.95 (295006) 12.5% ALC. **XD**

Today many winemakers are trying to make "serious" rosés, and too often these wines are reds in all but colour. Taste them blind and you'd think you were drinking red wine. This cabernet franc rosé is in a more familiar style, with vibrant, fresh, fruity flavours. It's dry and medium weight, with a crisp, clean texture. It goes well with roast ham or turkey, or summer salads.

NOTES
....
....
....
....

NEW!
★ ★ ★ ★

EastDell Summer Rosé 2013

VQA NIAGARA PENINSULA $12.95 (560243) 12% ALC. **M**

There's an attractive sweet-and-sour thing going on here, with a little sweetness in the fruit but a line of acidity adding a hint of tartness. It adds up to an easy-drinking and refreshing rosé that you can drink on its own or with chicken salad, fish burgers, or with many salads that have a dressing with a little sweetness. The wine is medium in weight and nicely balanced.

NOTES
....
....
....
....

Gran Feudo Rosado 2014

★ ★ ★ ★

DO NAVARRA $11.95 (165845) 13% ALC. **XD**

This rosé is made mainly from the garnacha tinta (black grenache) variety. After the grapes are pressed, the juice is left on the skins for 24 hours, just long enough for them to make the juice a bright pink colour. Apart from the hue, the texture and flavours are also attractive. It's a mid-weight, dry, well-balanced rosé, with good concentration and focus, and it goes well— all year round—with white fish and many poultry dishes.

NOTES
....
....
....
....

Henry of Pelham Rosé 2015
★ ★ ★ ★

VQA NIAGARA PENINSULA $14.95 (613471) 11.5% ALC. **XD**

Draws on half a dozen varieties (including zweigelt, pinot noir, and cabernet sauvignon) that change each year. It's well balanced and a fairly substantial rosé that you can drink on its own or pair successfully with roasted or grilled chicken or pork, and summer salads.

NOTES
....
....
....
....

Malivoire 'LadyBug' Rosé 2015
★ ★ ★ ★ ★

VQA NIAGARA PENINSULA $15.95 (559088) 12.5% ALC. **D**

[Vintages Essential] Malivoire's Lady Bug rosé—a blend of cabernet franc, gamay, and pinot noir—has been a hit for more than ten years. One of the earliest of the new generation of rosés, it's dry and almost full bodied, but it's definitively a rosé, not a red in pink clothing. Look for a great fruit-acid balance and a crisp texture, and enjoy this with baked ham or roast poultry.

NOTES
....
....
....
....

Ogier Ventoux Rosé 2015
★ ★ ★ ★

AOC VENTOUX $13.95 (134916) 13.5% ALC. **D**

A blend of grenache, syrah, and cinsault from the South of France, this is a dry rosé that drinks well on its own and pairs well with summer salads and roast chicken. Look for bright and nicely concentrated flavours paired with good acidity that translate to a crisp, clean texture.

NOTES
....
....
....
....

SPARKLING WINES & CHAMPAGNES

HERE'S THE DIFFERENCE BETWEEN CHAMPAGNE and sparkling wine: All champagnes are sparkling wines, but not all sparkling wines are champagnes. Champagne is a sparkling wine made in the Champagne region of France from specified grape varieties using a method defined by wine law. Sparkling wines made elsewhere (even if from the same grape varieties and in the same method) cannot be called champagne.

In this list, the sparkling wines are reviewed first, followed by the champagnes.

SPARKLING WINES

NEW!
★ ★ ★ ★

Acquesi Brachetto

DOC BRACHETTO, ITALY $13.10 (375667) 6.5% ALC.   M

[Non-vintage] Made from the brachetto grape variety in Piedmont, this sweet and fruity red sparkling wine is great for sipping in summer and also goes well with not-too-sweet fruit desserts. It's sweet, but not at all cloyingly so; think of a kir royal, and you'll get the style. The bubbles are spritzy and gentle, not nearly as assertive in most sparkling wines.

NOTES
....
....
....
....
....

★ ★ ★ ★

Astoria Prosecco

DOC PROSECCO, ITALY $15.05 (593855) 11% ALC.   D

[Non-vintage] Although many people think prosecco is a style of wine, it's a grape variety used to make sparkling wine in the northeastern corner of Italy. It tends to be off-dry, like this example, which is fruity and easy drinking. It's ideal for sipping before a meal, but you can also serve it with spicy food, as the sparkling fruitiness will help tone down the heat.

NOTES
....
....
....
....

NEW!
★ ★ ★ ★

Banero Prosecco

DOC PROSECCO, ITALY $14.90 (298489) 5.5% ALC.   M

[Vintages Essential][Kosher] Another prosecco in the ocean of that wine, but this one has merits beyond the fact that you can drink it at a seder. The fruit is well done—ripe but not too fruity, and better defined and structured than in most inexpensive proseccos. The acidity is refreshing, the bubbles plentiful, and the mousse (foam) gentle.

NOTES
....
....
....
....

NEW!
★ ★ ★ ★ ½
Bottega 'Il Vino dei Poeti' Prosecco 2015
DOC TREVISO, ITALY $14.95 (277202) 11.5% ALC.   D

This is a very attractive prosecco and it's vintage-dated, which is rare. It's very good to sip on its own or to drink with a broad range of foods. It goes well with prosciutto and melon, roast chicken, and grilled seafood and white fish, for example. The flavours are bright and fresh, the acidity is crisp and balanced, and there are ample fine bubbles. It's a very affordable sparkling rosé for celebrations.

NOTES
....
....
....
....

★ ★ ★ ★ ½
Cave Spring 'Blanc de Blancs' Brut Sparkling Wine
VQA NIAGARA ESCARPMENT, $29.95 (213983) 12% ALC.   D
ONTARIO

This lovely bottle of bubbles was made from chardonnay grapes (hence the reference to white grapes in 'Blanc de Blancs') in the traditional method used to make champagne. It shows stylish fruit that's defined and focused, supported by well-calibrated, refreshing acidity and enhanced by the streams of fine bubbles. It's fine drinking on its own or with seafood, shellfish, fish, poultry, and pork.

NOTES
....
....
....
....

★ ★ ★ ★
Château de Montgueret Brut Crémant de Loire
AOC CRÉMANT DE LOIRE, $19.95 (217760) 11.5% ALC.   D
FRANCE

[Non-vintage] This sparkling wine from the Loire Valley is made the same way as champagne. It's a lovely blend of chenin blanc, chardonnay, and cabernet franc. Slightly off-dry with attractive and complex flavours, it's an excellent aperitif that will perk up your appetite. Or pair it with spicy Asian dishes, especially seafood like garlic and ginger shrimp.

NOTES
....
....
....

Château des Charmes Brut Sparkling Wine

★ ★ ★ ★ ½

VQA NIAGARA-ON-THE-LAKE, ONTARIO $23.95 (224766) 12% ALC.   D

[Non-vintage] Made from chardonnay and pinot noir in the traditional method developed in Champagne, this is a lovely dry sparkling wine that delivers quality from start to finish. The flavours are pungent and nuanced with good concentration, and the acidity is bright and correct. There are plenty of bubbles, contributing to a finely grained, crisp mousse. Drink it alone or with poultry, pork, white fish, seafood, or smoked salmon.

NOTES

....

....

....

....

Codorníu Brut Classico Cava

★ ★ ★ ★ ★

DO CAVA, SPAIN $14.05 (215814) 11.5% ALC.   XD

[Non-vintage] Cava is made in the same way as champagne, which is to say that it goes through fermentation in the actual bottle you buy (rather than being bottled after the fermentation is complete). This is a very attractive example, with great flavours and a lovely crisp and balanced texture. It has plenty of small bubbles and a soft mousse. Sip it alone or serve it with spicy chicken, pork, or seafood.

NOTES

....

....

....

....

Codorníu 'Selección Raventos' Brut Rosé Cava

★ ★ ★ ★ ½

DO CAVA, SPAIN $16.95 (370080) 12% ALC.   XD

[Non-vintage] This is a delicious dry rosé sparkling wine that you can drink on its own or pair with foods such as poultry, patés, pork, and lighter pasta dishes. Made from pinot noir, it comes in a mid-depth, slightly dusty pink hue, and delivers plenty of bright, fresh fruit flavours. The acidity is vibrant, and there's no lack of fine bubbles, but they avoid the frothiness of too many inexpensive sparkling wines.

NOTES

....

....

....

SPARKLING WINES & CHAMPAGNES

NEW!
★ ★ ★ ★ ½

Cono Sur Rosé Sparkling Wine

DO BIO-BIO VALLEY, CHILE $13.95 (365205) 12% ALC.   D

The Bio-Bio Valley, one of the world's southernmost wine regions, gives
sunny days and cool nights, conditions that ripen the grapes and endow
them with the good level of acidity needed for sparkling wine. Made 100
percent from pinot noir grapes, this delivers lovely vibrant fruity flavours,
bright acidity, and plenty of bubbles. Drink it on its own or with poultry,
pork, and seafood.

NOTES

....

....

....

....

★ ★ ★ ★ ½

Cuvée 13 Rosé Sparkling Wine

VQA NIAGARA PENINSULA, $24.95 (147504) 12.5% ALC.   D
ONTARIO

[Vintages Essential] Made from pinot noir and chardonnay, using the
method employed in Champagne, this is a lovely sparkling rosé is very
versatile at the table. You can drink it on its own or pair it with fish,
seafood, poultry, and pork. It's dry, crisp and clean, with well-calibrated
fruit and balanced acidity, bright and serious fruit flavours, and plenty of
fine bubbles.

NOTES

....

....

....

....

NEW!
★ ★ ★ ★

David Rocco 'Dolce Vita' Prosecco

DOC PROSECCO, ITALY $14.95 (385906) 11% ALC.   D

This is an easy-drinking, quite fruity sparkling wine that you can sip on
its own or enjoy with spicy dishes featuring seafood or chicken. There's
a hint of sweetness on the palate, although the overall effect is dry, and
the acidity is crisp and clean. There are plenty of bubbles, making this a
refreshing aperitif you can easily bring to the table.

NOTES

....

....

....

De Chanceny Brut Rosé Crémant de Loire

★★★★ ½

AOC CRÉMANT DE LOIRE, FRANCE $18.80 (211466) 12.5% ALC.   **D**

[Non-vintage] A "crémant" is a sparkling wine from any one of a number of French wine regions. This one, a rosé, is from the Loire Valley, where it's 100 percent made from cabernet franc, and shows lively fruit flavours. The texture is crisp and clean and the bubbles are plentiful. This makes a fine sparkler to drink on its own, and goes well with roast turkey and cranberries.

NOTES

....

....

....

Freixenet 'Cordon Negro' Brut Cava

★★★★

DO CAVA, SPAIN $14.10 (216945) 11.5% ALC.   **D**

[Non-vintage] This is one of those reliable, versatile sparkling wines that you can count on, batch after batch. A blend of three grape varieties indigenous to Spain and made in the same way as champagne (it was fermented in the bottle you buy), it delivers lovely vibrant fruit flavours and has a zesty and refreshing texture. It has all the fizz you want for a special occasion, for an aperitif or for a spicy Asian dish. It's also available in 200 mL and 1.5 L bottles.

NOTES

....

....

....

Handsome Brut Sparkling Wine

★★★★

VQA NIAGARA PENINSULA, ONTARIO $19.20 (395160) 12% ALC.   **D**

[Non-vintage] It's a cute name and a successful fizz. Made in the "traditional" method, this delivers a clean, crisp, and lively texture, with plenty of small bubbles rising from the bottom of the glass. They produce a moderately firm mousse. The flavours are solid and nicely layered, and this is a sparkling wine you can enjoy on its own, as an aperitif, or take to the table.

NOTES

....

....

....

Henry of Pelham 'Cuvée Catharine' Brut Sparkling Wine

★ ★ ★ ★ ½

VQA NIAGARA PENINSULA,
ONTARIO

$29.95 (217521) 12% ALC. **XD**

[Non-vintage] Made from chardonnay and pinot noir, the two varieties most often used in champagne, this sparkling wine is dry, with a clean, crisp texture. The flavours are layered and defined, with a complex profile, and they're lifted by the vibrant acidity and steady streams of fine bubbles. The mousse is clean and crisp, and this is great with oysters, shellfish, and seafood in general, or as a partner to pork or white fish.

NOTES

Henry of Pelham 'Cuvée Catharine' Brut Rosé Sparkling Wine

★ ★ ★ ★ ½

VQA NIAGARA PENINSULA,
ONTARIO

$29.95 (217505) 12% ALC. **D**

[Non-vintage] This is a lovely sparkling rosé made from chardonnay and pinot noir by the method used in Champagne (although the winemaker is not permitted to express it that way on the label). You'll find very attractive vibrant fruit flavours here, echoed by the crisp, refreshing texture and fine bubbles. This is a lovely wine for the summer (or winter) table, and it's great for roast turkey, salads, and spicy dishes featuring chicken and seafood.

NOTES

Hungaria 'Grande Cuvée' Brut Sparkling Wine

★ ★ ★ ★ ½

HUNGARY

$12.85 (619288) 11.5% ALC. **D**

[Non-vintage] A very affordable sparkling wine, this is excellent on its own, as an aperitif, or with chicken, pork, or seafood—or use it as a base for mimosas or cocktails. It has solid, vibrant flavours, plenty of fizz and a moderate, soft mousse. It's dry and the texture is crisp and clean.

NOTES

Michelle Brut Sparkling Wine

★ ★ ★ ★ ½

WASHINGTON STATE $19.95 (363341) 11.5% ALC.   D

[Non-vintage] Although labelled simply by the state, the grapes are from Washington's Columbia Valley, and the varieties in the blend are chardonnay (63 percent), pinot noir (19 percent), and pinot gris (18 percent). The last adds to the lovely fruitiness, but this is dry, crisp, and shows lots of bubble action in the glass. Sip it on its own or enjoy it with smoked salmon or seafoods.

NOTES

....

....

....

....

Mionetto Treviso Prosecco

★ ★ ★ ★ ½

DOC TREVISO, ITALY $18.15 (266023) 11% ALC.   D

[Non-vintage] This is a quite elegant sparkling wine from the Treviso region near Venice. The flavours are very attractive—bright, vibrant, focused, and well defined—and the crisp acidity lightens them without undermining their intensity. There's a good level of fizz and a firm, soft mousse. It's great on its own, as an aperitif, or with many pork, poultry, and seafood dishes.

NOTES

....

....

....

....

Mumm Napa 'Brut Prestige' Sparkling Wine

★ ★ ★ ★

NAPA VALLEY, CALIFORNIA $25.95 (217273) 13% ALC.   D

[Non-vintage] French fizz tradition comes to California in this sparkling wine made in Napa (using the same grape varieties—pinot noir, chardonnay, and pinot meunier—as in champagne) by a famous champagne house. This is a great sparkling wine to drink as an aperitif— it has the crisp, mouth-watering texture that sets you up for food—or to enjoy with oysters. The flavours are complex and nuanced and the mousse is soft and defined.

NOTES

....

....

....

Paul Delane Réserve Brut Crémant de Bourgogne

★ ★ ★ ★ ½

AOC CRÉMANT DE BOURGOGNE, $19.95 (214981) 12% ALC. **D**
FRANCE

[Non-vintage] This well-balanced sparkling wine is made from four of Burgundy's permitted varieties: pinot noir, gamay, chardonnay, and aligoté. It has a crisp and clean texture from the bright acidity, concentrated flavours with a hint of toastiness, and streams of bubbles that end in a good mousse. Sip it on its own or drink it with grilled seafood, smoked salmon, or many spicy Asian dishes.

NOTES

Pierre Sparr Crémant d'Alsace Brut Réserve

★ ★ ★ ★ ½

AOC CRÉMANT D'ALSACE, $18.95 (388603) 12.5% ALC. **D**
FRANCE

[Non-vintage] Crémant d'Alsace is made by the "Traditional Method," using some of the approved grape varieties of Alsace, notably pinot blanc, pinot gris, and riesling. This example delivers lovely textured flavours from attack to finish, a crisp and clean texture, and plenty of bubble action. It's a sparkling wine you can enjoy as an aperitif or with poultry, seafood, and white fish.

NOTES

Santa Margherita Valdobbiadene Superiore Brut Prosecco

★ ★ ★ ★ ½

DOCG VALDOBBIADENE $18.95 (687582) 11.5% ALC. **XD**
PROSECCO SUPERIORE, ITALY

[Non-vintage] [Vintages Essential] Made in a brut (dry) style, this prosecco is a cut above many of its kind. It has the fruit richness of many proseccos, but it's a lot drier than most and shows more structure and complexity. You can drink this on its own, as an aperitif, or paired with a broad spectrum of foods from seafood, fish, and poultry, to pork and spicy Asian dishes.

NOTES

Segura Viudas Brut Reserva Cava

★ ★ ★ ★

DO CAVA, SPAIN $15.10 (216960) 12% ALC.   D

[Non-vintage] Made using the same method as champagne but from different grape varieties, this sparkling wine offers lovely, concentrated flavours and brisk acidity. You'll find streams of bubbles and a soft, attractive mousse. Like many dry sparkling wines it's extremely versatile on the table; you can pair it with poultry, seafood, fish, and spicy dishes (like many curries). Or serve it off the table as a wine to sip on its own.

NOTES

....

....

....

....

NEW!
★ ★ ★ ★ ½

Stone Dwellers Chardonnay–Pinot Noir Sparkling Wine

STRATHBOGIE RANGES, $11.95 (430074) 12% ALC.   D
AUSTRALIA

This lovely sparkling wine is a light amber colour, from contact with the pinot noir skins. And unlike the great majority of sparkling wines, it's sealed with a crown cap (like beer), making it very easy to open. The wine is very good indeed. There's plenty of flavour, good structure, and vibrant acidity, and there are streams of small bubbles. Enjoy this on its own or with poultry, pork, and many seafood dishes.

NOTES

....

....

....

....

Trapiche Extra Brut Sparkling Wine 2013

★ ★ ★ ★

MENDOZA, ARGENTINA $12.10 (262261) 12% ALC.   D

Made from chardonnay, semillon, and malbec grapes, this sparkling wine is dry with very attractive fruit flavours and is nicely structured and complex for the price. The acidity is crisp and clean, giving the wine fresh brightness, and there are plenty of quite fine bubbles. You can drink this on its own, pair it with fish, seafood, pork, and poultry, and it's inexpensive and good enough to use in cocktails.

NOTES

....

....

....

★ ★ ★ ★

Two Oceans Sauvignon Blanc Extra Dry Sparkling Wine

WO WESTERN CAPE,
SOUTH AFRICA
$7.45 (365353) 13% ALC.   **D**

This light and fruity sparkling wine is an easy choice for sipping on its own or taking to the table, where it pairs well with seafood, chicken, white fish, pork, and many vegetarian dishes. The flavours are attractive right through, and the sauvignon acidity is vibrant and refreshing. The bubbles are small and abundant.

NOTES

....

....

....

NEW!
★ ★ ★ ★

Villa Maria Lightly Sparkling Sauvignon Blanc 2015

NEW ZEALAND
$17.95 (429969) 13% ALC.   **D**

New in the LCBO, this is a lovely variation on both New Zealand sauvignon blanc and on sparkling wine. It's definitely New Zealand sauvignon, but the bubbles lighten the flavours and make it that much more refreshing. And it's definitely sparkling, but in a more gentle way than most. With well-defined fruit, good acidity, and a drink-more quality, it's great for sipping on its own or with seafood and fish appetizers.

NOTES

....

....

....

....

★ ★ ★ ★

Villa Sandi Prosecco

DOC PROSECCO TREVISO, ITALY $14.60 (394387) 11% ALC.   **D**

From the Treviso sub-region of the broader prosecco region, this is a solid sparkling wine that's dry but fruity enough to enjoy on its own. Alternatively, it pairs well with many summer salads. The flavours are fresh and bright, the acidity is crisp and refreshing, and there's plenty of bubble action in the glass. In short, it delivers all you want from an affordable sparkling wine.

NOTES

....

....

....

....

CHAMPAGNES

NEW!
★ ★ ★ ★

G.H. Mumm 'Cordon Rouge' Brut Champagne

AOC CHAMPAGNE $59.95 (308056) 12% ALC.   D

Mumm "Cordon Rouge" was the first champagne I ever drank (in New Caledonia, while I was in high school). So it has nostalgia value, but I continue to enjoy it for its quality, too. It has a bright, substantial feel to it, and is very drinkable. The flavours are multifaceted, the acidity is crisp and clean, and the bubbles perform well. Enjoy it on its own or with many seafood dishes.

NOTES

....

....

....

★ ★ ★ ★ ★

Louis Roederer 'Brut Premier' Champagne

AOC CHAMPAGNE $71.95 (268771) 12% ALC.   XD

This is a fine champagne that speaks quality and elegance from start to finish. The flavours are well defined and focused, with good complexity and structure. They're more than ably supported by a broad seam of crisp, fresh acidity. The bubbles are fine, the beads are persistent, and the mousse is firm and generous. It's a champagne for the table, where it goes well with fish, seafood, pork, and poultry.

NOTES

....

....

....

....

★ ★ ★ ★ ½

Perrier-Jouët 'Grand Brut' Brut Champagne

AOC CHAMPAGNE $69.75 (155341) 12% ALC.   D

[Non-vintage] This is a really lovely champagne that sizzles on its own or in the company of food. The flavours are rich, tiered, and well focused, and the texture is crisp and elegant. Here you find a winning tension between the brisk acidity and the roundness of the fruit, with hints of lees (dead yeast cells) flickering between. This is a fine aperitif, and it goes well with many seafood, fish, poultry, and pork dishes.

NOTES

....

....

....

Piper-Heidsieck Brut Champagne

★ ★ ★ ★ ½

AOC CHAMPAGNE $59.85 (462432) 12% ALC.   **D**

[Non-vintage] This is a versatile champagne. You can pop the cork (not literally—always ease the cork from a bottle of sparkling wine so that it opens with a gentle hiss, not a pop) to celebrate birthdays and the like, or serve it with chicken, turkey, or pork. Dry and medium bodied with solid, complex flavours, and a refreshing texture, it shows fine streams of bubbles that make for a clean, crisp mousse.

NOTES

....

....

....

....

Pol Roger 'Extra Cuvée de Réserve' Brut Champagne

★ ★ ★ ★ ½

AOC CHAMPAGNE $66.05 (217158) 12.5% ALC.   **XD**

[Non-vintage] This is a very good-quality champagne at a very good price. It has everything you look for in the animal: solid fruit flavours, complexity, a crisp and zesty texture, lots of fine bubbles streaming up from the bottom of the glass, and an edgy but quite soft mousse in the mouth. It's ideal as an aperitif, but you can take it to the table and drink it with Asian cuisine or seafood, fish, poultry, and pork dishes.

NOTES

....

....

....

....

Taittinger 'Brut Réserve' Champagne

★ ★ ★ ★ ½

AOC CHAMPAGNE $60.65 (365312) 12.5% ALC.   **D**

Taittinger is a well-known champagne house, and for good reason. This example, made from pinot noir and chardonnay, is quite elegant in style, with well-defined and focused fruit flavours and a crisp, zesty texture from the supporting acidity. Fine bubbles rise in beads, and the mousse is both firm and yielding. This is a very good champagne for food, and it goes well with many fish, seafood, and poultry dishes.

NOTES

....

....

....

....

Tarlant 'Brut Réserve' Champagne

★ ★ ★ ★ ½

AOC CHAMPAGNE $43.50 (325167) 12% ALC. D

[Non-vintage] This is a quality champagne priced so that you can drink it on occasions that are special simply because you have a bottle and feel like opening it. It's for sipping on its (and your) own on a "champagne Sunday," or for taking to the table with poultry or pork dishes. In any event, it's long on flavours (including a lovely yeasty note) and complexity, with crisp freshness, fine bubbles, and a generous mousse.

NOTES

....

....

....

....

Victoire 'Prestige' Brut Champagne

★ ★ ★ ★ ★

AOC CHAMPAGNE $39.95 (190025) 12% ALC. XD

[Non-vintage] This is a very good price for the quality. The texture is crisp and bright, with good complexity and yeast notes, and the flavours are nicely layered and consistent right through the palate. It throws plenty of fine bubbles, forms a firm but gentle mousse, and is great sipped on its own, as an aperitif, or with white meats and fish.

NOTES

....

....

....

....

SWEET &
DESSERT WINES

ALL DESSERT WINES ARE SWEET, but not all sweet wines are suitable for dessert. For example, icewine, which is a style Ontario is famous for, is often too sweet for desserts but goes well with foie gras (which is normally served as an appetizer or part of a main course) and blue cheese. This list includes a number of sweet wines, and I've suggested what goes best with each.

★ ★ ★ **Batasiolo 'Bosc dla Rei' Moscato d'Asti 2013**

DOCG MOSCATO D'ASTI, ITALY $15.65 (277194) 5.5% ALC. **S**

Made from the moscato variety, this is a luscious, moderately sweet wine that goes well with cheesecakes and fruit pies. It has a round texture allied to good acidity, and is very lightly viscous. It would also go well with foie gras or a cheese course that included not-too-strong blue cheeses.

NOTES

....

....

....

....

★ ★ ★ ★ ½ **Cave Spring 'Indian Summer' Select Late Harvest Riesling 2013**

VQA NIAGARA PENINSULA, $24.95 (415901) 12.5% ALC. **S**
ONTARIO

[Vintages Essential, 375 mL] This is not icewine, although the grapes were partly frozen when picked. They were left on the vine past the usual harvest date to shrivel and lose water, then picked after the first frost. The result is a wine with sweet—but not very sweet—flavours that are complex and delicious, complemented by vibrant acidity. It's lovely to drink by itself, but you can serve it (chilled) with any fruit-based dessert that's no sweeter than the wine.

NOTES

....

....

....

....

★ ★ ★ ★ ★ **Domaine Pinnacle Cidre de Glace/Ice Cider**

QUEBEC $25.65 (94094) 12% ALC. **S**

[375mL] This is one of two fruit wines (not made from grapes) in this book, and it's a beauty. Ice cider is made in a way similar to icewine, by freezing the fruit to separate its water from the juice. The result here is a rich, sweet, slightly viscous wine that has distinct apple and some honeyed flavours. Just as important, it has the bright acidity to keep the sweetness in check. Drink it with not-too-sweet fruit (especially apple) desserts.

NOTES

....

....

....

Henry of Pelham Riesling Icewine 2014

★ ★ ★ ★ ★

VQA NIAGARA PENINSULA, ONTARIO $49.95 (430561) 9% ALC. S

[Vintages Essential, 375 mL] This is an icewine that delivers the best in the style. It has all the sweetness that shrivelled and frozen grapes can produce, but it's nuanced and layered. Meanwhile, the threat of a cloying, teeth-hurting experience is averted by the nice line of acidity. It's a more drinkable icewine than many, and for this reason you could chill it slightly (about 15 minutes in the fridge), then sip it by itself or drink it with foie gras or briny blue cheese.

NOTES

Henry of Pelham Special Select Late Harvest Vidal 2013

★ ★ ★ ★ ½

VQA ONTARIO $19.95 (395228) 10.8% ALC. S

[375 mL] This stylish wine is made from selected vidal grapes from bunches left on the vines well after the normal harvest period. With concentrated sugar, they have produced a luscious wine that goes well with sweet, fruit-based desserts, briny blue cheese, or seared foie gras. The dense and focused sweet flavours are balanced by brisk and vibrant acidity that cuts through the sweetness and ensures it's not cloying.

NOTES

Inniskillin Vidal Icewine 2014

★ ★ ★ ★

VQA NIAGARA PENINSULA, ONTARIO $49.95 (551085) 10% ALC. S

[Vintages Essential, 375 mL] Inniskillin is arguably the world's best-known icewine producer. They make icewine from a number of grape varieties, and this vidal version delivers all the rich, pungent sweetness you buy icewine for, effectively offset by a seam of vibrant acidity. It gives the wine a sort of juiciness that enables you to enjoy it on its own, with blue cheese or with foie gras.

NOTES

★ ★ ★ ★

Ironstone 'Obsession' Symphony 2013

CALIFORNIA $15.10 (295931) 12% ALC.   M

This is a sweet (but not too sweet) wine made from the symphony grape
variety, an aromatic cross of muscat of Alexandria and grenache gris. The
flavours are intense and pungent, but a good dose of acidity takes care of
much of the sweetness. (Think of a fairly rich gewürztraminer.) Chilled to
bring out the acidity, this is a good partner for many spicy Asian dishes.

NOTES

....

....

....

....

★ ★ ★ ★ ½

Southbrook Framboise

ONTARIO $17.95 (341024) 14% ALC.   S

[Non-vintage, 375 mL] This is one of two fruit (non-grape) wines in
this book. Southbrook's framboise, made from the royalty variety of
raspberries and fortified with a little brandy, has become an icon, so it's
here. It's full of rich, intense, sweet flavours, and the viscous texture has
the acidity to cut through the sweetness. Drink it with rich chocolate
desserts or pour it over ice cream. Amazing!

NOTES

....

....

....

....

FORTIFIED WINES

FORTIFIED WINES ARE WINES whose alcohol level has been raised, and style modified, by the addition of brandy or a neutral, distilled alcohol. The best-known fortified wines are port and sherry.

Port is a sweet, fortified wine (usually red, sometimes white) made in the Douro region of Portugal. It's generally served after dinner with dessert, cheese, or nuts, or on its own, and some people like the combination of port and a cigar. Port can also be served as an aperitif, a common practice in France. Although other countries produce fortified wines labelled "port," the name is properly reserved for the wine produced in the Douro region according to the rules set out for port production there.

Sherry is a fortified wine made in Jerez, a wine region in the south of Spain. It comes in many styles, from clear, crisp, light, and dry, to black, heavy, viscous, and sweet. You'll find other fortified wines labelled sherry, but only fortified wine from the Jerez region made in a designated way can properly be called sherry. Although sherry is fortified and is generally drunk as an aperitif, it is also a very successful partner for food, and the spectrum of styles is broad enough that it's possible to find a sherry for any dish.

★★★★ ½ **Ferreira 'Dona Antonia' Reserva Tawny Porto**
DOC PORTO $18.95 (157586) 20% ALC. **S**

Named for the head of the Ferreira port-producing family from the early
nineteenth century, this is a luscious port. It delivers sweet, rich, multi-
layered flavours and a texture that's quite viscous and seems to swell in
your mouth. But the acidity clicks in and kills the sweetness, leaving you
with a fruity and complex finish. It's delicious on its own or with blue
cheese and roasted nuts.

NOTES
....
....
....

★★★★ **Fonseca 'Bin No. 27' Reserve Port**
DOC PORTO $16.95 (325506) 20% ALC. **M**

This is a quite luscious port, with the rich and layered textures and
fruit flavours you expect. They play right through the palate and into a
long finish, while the acidity keeps the extremes in check and makes it
drinkable. Sip this on its own as a digestif, or enjoy it with chocolates,
strongly flavoured blue cheeses, or dried fruit.

NOTES
....
....
....
....

★★★★ ½ **Graham's 20-Year Tawny Port**
DOC PORTO $38.40 (620641) 20% ALC. **M**

[500 mL] To be labelled as "10-year" or "20-year," ports don't need to
spend that long in oak barrels; they need to achieve the quality and style a
port typically would if it did. But these ports do have long aging, and this
one shows it in its structure and the complexity and depth of its flavours.
It's elegant, smooth and best appreciated on its own, at least for the first
few sips. Then bring on the Stilton cheese.

NOTES
....
....
....
....

Sandeman Late Bottled Vintage Port 2009

★ ★ ★

DOC PORTO $17.15 (195974) 20% ALC. **S**

True to its name, this port from the 2009 vintage was bottled in 2013.
It's a classic LBV, with depth and intensity of flavour and texture. Lightly
viscous, it shows plenty of complexity as it moves through the palate, and
is well balanced and nicely tannic. Port is one of the rare wines that go
with chocolate (dark and bitter), so indulge!

NOTES

....

....

....

....

....

Taylor Fladgate 20-Year-Old Tawny Port

★ ★ ★ ★ ★

DOC PORTO $69.95 (149047) 20% ALC. **S**

[Vintages Essential] This port has been aged in oak for twenty years
before being bottled. Over that time, it has developed layers and layers of
flavours that emerge within the essentially sweet port profile. The acidity
is right-on, lightening the wine and making a second (and third) glass
effortless. You can drink this on its own or with a cigar and/or a stilton or
stilton-like cheese.

NOTES

....

....

....

....

Taylor Fladgate 'First Estate' Reserve Port

★ ★ ★ ★ ½

DOC PORTO $17.15 (309401) 20% ALC. **S**

This is made in a slightly less-sweet style than most ports. There are some
red wines described as port-like because they're so rich, intense, and
sweet, and if you think of those, this port is just across the line, in a style
approaching red wine. Being less sweet, it's easier drinking and goes well
with aged cheeses (like very old, crumbly cheddar). The texture here is
intense and rich, but it leaves a drying sensation in your mouth.

NOTES

....

....

....

....

Warre's 'Otima' 10-Year Port

★ ★ ★ ★

DOC PORTO $22.20 (566174) 20% ALC. S

[500 mL] If you think of port as an after-dinner drink, with the colour and weight of the leather armchairs favoured by the crusty old guys who drink it, try Otima. It's made in a lighter style—as you might expect from the colour of this port, which is paler than most—but it still has lovely sweet fruit flavours. You can chill it as an aperitif or drink it at room temperature after dinner.

NOTES

....
....
....
....

SHERRIES

★ ★ ★ ★ **Alvear Fino**

DOC MONTILLA-MORILES $12.75 (112771) 15% ALC. **D**

[Non-vintage] This isn't technically a sherry, as it isn't made in Jerez, in southern Spain. Montilla, the region next to Jerez, produces wines in the same styles as sherry, from delicate and bone dry to rich and sweet. This one is on the delicate and dry end of the spectrum. It's crisp and refreshing, with a light body, and it goes well with salty Spanish tapas like olives and grilled octopus.

NOTES
....
....
....
....

★ ★ ★ ★ **Croft Original Fine Pale Cream Sherry**

DO JEREZ $15.95 (73452) 17.5% ALC. **M**

This is a slightly sweet sherry but with a resolutely dry undertone. The sweetness comes through more on the finish than through the palate. Served chilled, it's a very good sipping drink on a hot day (but watch the alcohol), or you can pair it with many tapas-style appetisers, such as olives, grilled nuts, salty cheeses, and cured meats.

NOTES
....
....
....
....

NEW!
★ ★ ★ ★ ★ **Lustau 'Don Nuño' Oloroso Sherry**

DO JEREZ $15.65 (375105) 20% ALC. **M**

Rated as Medium by the LCBO, I would think it's Dry. There's a touch of sweetness on the attack, but it disappears by mid-palate and gives way to a range of mature flavours and rancio dimensions that are just lovely to taste. On the finish it's quite astringent. This is a real pleasure to sip on its own, but you can enjoy it with many tapas, including olives, fish, and meats.

NOTES
....
....
....
....

★ ★ ★ ★ ★

Lustau 'Los Arcos' Amontillado Sherry

DO JEREZ   **$15.35** (375097) **18.5% ALC.** **XD**

This is a dry style of sherry with a little fruitiness alongside the classic rancio character. It's dominated by dried fruit flavours, with a broad seam of diffuse, clean acidity. Chill this down and sip it on its own or pair it with many Spanish tapas: olives, fish, spicy sausages, ham, and the like.

NOTES

....

....

....

....

★ ★ ★ ★ ★

Tio Pepe Extra Dry Fino Sherry

DO JEREZ   **$17.95** (231829) **15% ALC.** **D**

[Non-vintage] Tio Pepe is an iconic fino sherry. Made in an astringently dry style ("extra dry" is an understatement!), it has pungent, high-toned flavours backed by bright, taut acidity. It's not to everyone's taste when drunk on its own, but it's an excellent partner for many Spanish tapas dishes such as olives, stuffed vine leaves, almonds, grilled octopus, and chorizo.

NOTES

....

....

....

....

NOTES

NOTES

NOTES

NOTES

NOTES

ABOUT THE AUTHOR

Rod Phillips is a wine author, historian, journalist, and judge who lives in Ottawa. He is wine columnist for the *Ottawa Citizen* and wine writer and contributing editor of *NUVO* magazine. He contributes to newspapers, magazines, podcasts, and other wine media in Canada, the US, and Europe. He writes occasionally for *Vines,* Canada's leading wine magazine, and has written extensively for *The World of Fine Wine* (UK). Apart from *The 500 Best-Value Wines in the LCBO,* he is the author of *Alcohol: A History* (2014), a global history of alcoholic drinks, and *French Wine: A History* (2016), which surveys wine in France from the first vineyards to the present.

Rod is wine advisor to the Ottawa Wine & Food Festival, and co-chair of the Ottawa Wine Challenge. He has judged wine competitions in Canada, Europe, South America, and New Zealand, is a member of the CBC Radio Ottawa wine panel, and occasionally gives wine classes. He was the curator of an exhibition on the history of Canadian wine at the Canadian Museum of Civilization (2004–5), was named Wine Journalist of the Year at the 2007 Ontario Wine Awards, and received the Award of Excellence for 2012 from Drinks Ontario, the association of wine and spirits agents and importers. He regularly visits wine regions and wineries around the world.

Rod publishes the *WinePointer* biweekly newsletter, which reviews wines available at the LCBO and Vintages and elsewhere in Ontario. You can subscribe to the newsletter (it's free) on his website, rodphillipsonwine.com. You can also follow him on Twitter at @rodphillipswine and contact him at rodphillips@worldsofwine.com.